ASIA Entrepreneurship Wealth Creation with E-commerce Business

ASIA Entrepreneurship Wealth Creation with E-commerce Business

E-Commerce Business Entrepreneurship

K.K. Mani

PARTRIDGE

To order additional copies of this book, contact
Toll Free 800 101 2657 (Singapore)
Toll Free 1 800 81 7340 (Malaysia)
orders.singapore@partridgepublishing.com

www.partridgepublishing.com/singapore

Table of Contents

Wealth

What is "Wealth"

Wealth measures the estimation of the considerable number of advantages of worth claimed by a man, group, organization or nation. Wealth is controlled by taking the aggregate market estimation of all physical and elusive resources claimed, at that point subtracting all obligations. Basically, Wealth is the collection of assets. Particular individuals, associations and countries are said to be affluent when they can aggregate numerous profitable assets or products.

Separating "Wealth"

Wealth is communicated in an assortment of ways. For people, total assets is the most widely recognized articulation of Wealth, while nations measure by (GDP), or GDP per capita.

What Constitutes Wealth

View of what constitutes Wealth changes after some time among social orders. The antiquated ancient origins once had a money related framework in light of wheat. A few societies have utilized wares, for example, rice and salt set up of cash now and again. Inuit and Eskimo social orders exchanged seal oil and lard, which they could eat as sustenance, or consume as fuel to give light and warmth. African and Native American tribes once exchanged with wampum and shells, and utilized those as the premise of their money related frameworks. Heads of dairy cattle and domesticated animals are as yet utilized as mediums of trade in a few societies.

Gold and silver are valuable metals and significant items that have shaped the premise of the money related frameworks in numerous nations. Be that as it may, the costs of gold and silver were liable to fluctuating value valuations and once in a while stayed stable for long stretches. Amid World War II, the administration prohibited the private responsibility for. Financial specialists have contended for a considerable length of time about tying the estimation of an administration's cash to its gold and silver stores.

Measuring Wealth

Cash is the most widely recognized, but defective, methods for measuring Wealth. The estimation of an item or material utilized as the reason for a money related framework relies upon the amount others will exchange or give work in return to it. Another factor is the level of all-inclusive acknowledgment the material or product has. On the off chance that nobody outside a group will acknowledge the cash in return for merchandise or administrations, it has no an incentive outside of the general public that utilizations it.

The degree to which outside powers can control the estimation of cash can dramatically affect measuring Wealth. One of the real issues with paper money is that it is liable to control and cheapening by the demonstrations of one or a couple of people through falsifying and deceitful exchanging. Another issue is that it is moderately simple for governments and banks to control the estimation of cash by printing progressively and making it simple to get, or by printing less and expanding credit limitations. Therefore, money related instruments and ventures, land, assets and even domesticated animals can be utilized to gauge and assess Wealth.

Online Business Wealth Creation

> **Regard your online business as though it were a flourishing disconnected business.**

How would you treat your online business? Do you consider it to be a pastime? Something amusing to do in your extra time?

It may be anything but difficult to see it that way, particularly on the off chance that it isn't winning you a great many dollars yet. In any case, in the event that you truly want to develop it into a huge business, you have to go about as though it is now.

A way of life business is pleasant to have, yet understand that you can make considerably more prominent Wealth by concentrating on the continuous development of your business. Try not to stick around for your dare to feel like a major business. Consider the choices you would make on the off chance that it as of now was.

Locate the correct programming for your business, we are end to end internet business supplier at BiggyBox.my

As an entrepreneur, you need the profundity of vision to see potential issues previously they even come up. For some online business entrepreneurs, programming is something that should be tended to and assessed on a continuous premise, since it's truly foundational to the whole operation.

Security concerns, adaptability, ease of use, advertising instruments and different variables must be considered when you're searching for the correct programming to depend on.

The correct apparatus depends to a great extent on what needs you have. Try to distinguish your difficulties and do your exploration to discover the device that matches your necessities.

Make sense of where your clients are.

This is business 101. Know who your intended interest group is, and make sense of where they get a kick out of the chance to hang out. Numerous entrepreneurs don't make this stride genuinely, and wind up squandering a great deal of their opportunity and assets on promoting that doesn't change over.

Be that as it may, you do need to consider this rule important. On the off chance that you can make sense of where you're advertising dollars will create the best rate of profitability, you'll have a less demanding time getting a constant flow of leads.

Enable your clients to be your image ministers.

There's nothing very like the shining tribute of a fulfilled client to add believability to your business. By gathering and sharing tributes and audits all the time, you can support more deals from your site guests.

"The most capable tip we could give in becoming your online business is enabling your clients to be your image envoys," and "Make it simple to incorporate and share tributes and surveys from your clients."

You can talk yourself up as much as you need, however it's at last what individuals say in regards to your business that will have the greatest effect on purchasing choices. Your clients are the best resources you have, so figure out how to use them.

Expel rubbing from the checkout procedure.

In the event that you need to offer more item, you need to guarantee that your guests aren't getting disappointed, relinquishing their trucks and departing your site to discover another store where they can buy a contender item.

Erosion is one of the greatest difficulties for most retailers, particularly as we move into the versatile age. You need to figure out how to make checkout so straightforward and simple that anybody could do it. Dispense with the requirement for account creation. Lessen the quantity of screens the client needs to experience. Ensure your default shipping choice is the least expensive, unless there's a speedier choice at a similar cost. Use as few shape fields as could reasonably be expected, and utilize auto-fill where appropriate. Spare charging, delivery and installment data when and where conceivable.

Give a few approaches to your clients to pay for their request, including regular installment alternatives, for example, PayPal and BiggyPay.

Entrepreneurship

On the off chance that we take a gander at business enterprise regarding phenomenal esteem creation and catch, which I do, at that point unmistakably esteem can be made and caught in an expansive assortment of routes, and there is no from the earlier motivation to think doing this without any preparation by means of a start-up is the main or even the most ideal way. Remarkable esteem creation may include procuring, re-purposing, turning off, or recombining underutilized or underestimated resources. Over the previous decade or something like that, look reserves have turned into a successful vehicle for gaining underestimated organizations to implant with capital, administration and development. Privately-run companies, extensive partnerships, R&D focuses and colleges — any of these can be fundamental in making or arranging for resources rich with undiscovered potential.

Exceptional esteem creation can't happen without development, and entrepreneurial development post start-up has various difficulties which can be a request of greatness more troublesome than basically beginning a wander. Development involves building up an intense deals and showcasing machine, assembling an association by procuring and overseeing various gatherings of individuals, and knowing how to get vital information sources, for example, the correct sorts of capital and providers. Development requires astounding measures of vitality and commitment, also smarts. Forward-looking approach, and additionally culture and the private part, must help every one of these abilities and assets more than it does at display.

So it is a few seconds ago unfolding on numerous in business and government that when these start-up programs are effective in animating endeavor birth as opposed to wander scale, the enormous difficulties of development may incomprehensibly turn out to be more awful, worse, and can leave numerous stale or exaggerated endeavors that may have minimal genuine prospect of development.

We can refocus approach on scale-up in various ways. One is basic: quit regarding wander survival as a pointer of arrangement achievement and begin taking a gander at those that develop. It is additionally important for strategy to encourage to a great degree abnormal amounts of wander passing and reusing so as to stay away from a plenty of valueless new companies. Concentrate significantly more consideration on improving the neighborhood work pool, a fundamental part of a successful biological system. Business visionaries I meet with from Silicon Valley to Mumbai to Rio De Ji Rio who have prevailing with regards to getting market footing generally whine about the lack of properly talented individuals and supervisors to procure. Entrepreneurial endeavors can never develop without ability, and the two essential sorts of ability required — new managers and new workers — must advance together.

Moreover (and here is the place the child rearing similarity separates), involvement and the current information propose that few high-development endeavors might be adequate to produce the majority of the social and monetary advantages of business. One wander which develops to 100 individuals in five years is likely more advantageous (to business visionaries, investors, workers, and governments alike) than 50 which stagnate at two. Attempt has as of late demonstrated that only a few surprisingly scaling endeavors can have a totally unbalanced effect on many successors, and effect the business enterprise culture in a district. Which is more critical, conceiving an offspring or bringing up kids? Clearly, birth is vital, yet it is incredibly deficient. In concentrating business enterprise strategy solely on new companies we are favoring amount of start-up to the detriment of nature of scale-up.

Basic Rule Millionaire MindSet

You ought to get rich; it is your duty to get rich– means you might . . .

> Provide a useful product or service

> Trusted with money; yes, most wealthy people are honest and nice

> Attract people and develop great enterprises

> Serve the community and mankind

Programming leads to your thoughts

Thoughts lead to your feelings

Feelings lead to your actions

Actions lead to your

What We Want You to Get From This

Take a proactive role in planning, goal setting, and personal evaluation.

Get out there and do it. Take the initiative and have a bias toward action. Get experience however you can, build your network, have confidence, and be in it to win.

Write down your goals. Aim high. Shoot for the sky and you'll land on the tree tops.

Review & revise your goals monthly, keeping track of all setbacks and progress.

Products

You can manage all of your products and variants from the Products area of BiggyBox.

Products are goods or services that you and/or your sellers sell on your store. Your store is defined by the products that you sell hence; hence product management is very important for your store. Within the products panel you can manage the entire product range in a very smooth and systematic manner.

Products

Products are goods or services that you and/or your sellers sell on your store. Your store is defined by the products that you sell hence, hence product management is very important for your store. Within the products panel you can manage the entire product range in a very smooth and systematic manner.

Click on Products in the side panel on the left to access products section.

Within the products section there are different subsections related to products.

Products

Add single product, import products in bulk, or perform common operations on products e.g. edit or duplicate them; delete a single or multiple products at one go, publish or unpublish products. You can also search and filter products.

Categories

You can create Categories to segregate products into different segments. BiggyBox allows multi level categories to allow hierarchical organization of your products. For example, "Clothes", "Clothes > Men", "Clothes > Men > Casuals" could be possible categories.

Brands

You can manage the Brands that your products belong to. On your storefront, you can show a brands page and you an also have dedicate pages for each of the brands.

Collections

Collections can be used to group products across different categories together e.g. "Featured Products"

Option Sets

Option Sets is used to give behavior to product options. For example, you can define if you want the color option to be displayed as dropdown, swatch, radio or any other way.

Reviews

Analyze and manage reviews of your products.

Advanced commercial centers will be above all else

Advanced commercial centers are new to the B2B space in retail, however appropriation of more visual, cooperative and social devices will definitely increment in current/not so distant future. Retailers will shop simply like buyers in these associated B2B commercial centers, accelerating and streamlining monotonous and oppressive backend forms and at last show signs of improvement items to showcase speedier.

Internet Protection will be a noteworthy concern

With purchaser like, social innovations becoming the overwhelming focus one year from now, the utilization of devices like Pinterest and Instagram for gathering restrictive thoughts will decrease among the retail group. Groups will understand the dangers of utilizing open systems to house outlines and motivation. Rather, computerized installment arrangements and planners will work together with their legitimate groups to ensure they have solid frameworks set up for network assurance.

Social will Rise on the Backend

The item improvement process will be less about purchasing pens, paper and other physical things and more about purchasing and sharing thoughts. As the retail group teams up and use the information, skill and encounters of everyone around them, they'll have the capacity to better motivate and make awesome items that shoppers really need to purchase.

Joint effort is the name of the amusement and if retailers can't use this to move at the speed in which they think, everything backs off, from item outline and advancement to the production network and deals. This implies completely taking advantage of the groups retail groups communicate with consistently and utilizing the advances available to them to safely convey the most incentive to their client base.

Extraordinary item is the backbone of a retail business and in a world that is loaded with players of every single diverse sort and sizes; it doesn't take much for customers to lose intrigue. Retailers will at last comprehend the vital part joint effort plays in their prosperity one year from now and will begin to end up noticeably more tribal, visual and intuitive, eventually helping them outline and convey incredible items and administrations that emerge.

Current year established the framework for retail advancement and development. It's dependent upon us to expand on this energy in and genuinely grasp the social, associated world we live in so we can see achievement in current/not so distant future and past.

Step by step instructions to Avoid Getting control the ecommerce business by Famous B2B2C Provider This Holiday Season

Current year has been the time of client experience. This Christmas season, retailers will feel the full impacts of the omnichannel client travel center. Buyers anticipate that a consistent way will buy, paying little respect to gadget or area, and for retailers to contend with online monsters like B2B2C leaders amid the busiest shopping period of the year, brands need to convey only that.

The key to a quick, easy to use, m-and internet business encounter is a completely coordinated frontend-to-backend omnichannel setup, yet to accomplish it retailers need to consider three key variables while setting up their channels – both toward the front look and believe and back-end bolster capacities - for the occasion surge:

The Customer Knowledge

Do you know their identity? Have they marked into your portable web or local application? What level of clients is known versus unknown? Reliable client encounters over all touchpoints depend on knowing precisely who the client is and customizing the substance to their socioeconomics, purchasing practices and needs.

Focusing on essentially in view of geolocation and time of day may have been sufficient for last Christmas season however this year will rotate around individualized, individual adventures for every shopper. Retailers need to investigate the information they are gathering about their clients and where they can make a move to convey a more client driven and conduct based understanding. Without the profound comprehension of clients and their shopping designs, retailers will be flying visually impaired when endeavoring to make an affair that drives transformations.

The Consistent Experience

Albeit the sum total of what retailers have been presented to the expression "omnichannel" at this point yet most have not aced implementing a viable omnichannel encounter. Conveying and organizing what encounters will be offered over the distinctive touchpoints will give you a chance to distinguish potential ranges of irregularity. You will likewise need to guarantee that any personalization or item proposal instrument is not particular to only one a player in the experience, as you may invest superfluous energy and cash making a sorted out and inconvenient UX. The look and feel of the experience is a substantial factor toward the front, yet the back-end usefulness assumes an equivalent part in how the shopper sees the general collaboration with the brand.

Portable Conversion Rates Successful Over Holiday Season

Inquiry promoting organization of a marketplace has finished its examination of the add and flow year season shopping, incorporating the discoveries into its ebb and flow year Holiday Season: By the Numbers report. The information shows that contrasted with past year add up to internet business occasion deals expanded by double digit %.

Marketplace additionally found that buys on cell phones, also called e-Commerce, outperformed 30% in current year. These discoveries coordinate Marketplace's guage occasion web based business figures, which were discharged in September year to year.

While we sought after better deals figures, we are satisfied that we could anticipate the occasion online business deals figures so precisely. We described the moderate development figures this year to a few variables like sooner than common Christmas shopping with major online occasions like B2B2C leaders's Special Day, customers utilizing their cell phones to buy yet making more affordable buys on portable, and to the dubious political condition."

Marketplace broke down the internet business deals information by INTERNATIONAL. areas and found the most noteworthy increment in the mainstream region with a 19.9% expansion. The following most noteworthy was found in the tier 2 region with 9.5%, at that point in focal INTERNATIONAL. with 6.5% and afterward the upper tier 2 region with 5.8%.

Hunt advertising patterns were likewise followed in the report. Impressions saw the greatest lift this year with an expansion of 35.7% and transformations expanded by 18.63%. The normal cost-per-click went up by only 1.56% and the normal request esteem diminished by 5.4%.

The most prevalent time of day to purchase was amid the evening hours of 12 p.m. to 8 p.m. what's more, the second most well known time amid the morning hours of 6 a.m. to 12 p.m. A similar time of day insights likewise connected to impressions and snaps.

"The uptick in versatile movement this festival season made changes and impressions increment reasonably significantly, however caused general interest to diminish as individuals commonly spend less on their cell phones than on desktops," proceeded with Bose. "The season of day rates are likewise imperative discoveries for retailers as they get ready for future computerized showcasing efforts, which ought to be centered around the evening hours when buyers are demonstrating the most engagement and purpose to buy."

Maintaining a strategic distance from IT Outages amid the Holiday Season Responsive Design: Friend or Foe?

The festival shopping season is for all intents and purposes upon us, and online retailers would prefer not to persevere through any IT downtime amongst Chinese New Year, Diwali and Ramadan when many ring up 33% of their yearly receipts.

That is a considerable measure of green. Web based shopping baskets should enlist almost $100 billion this Christmas season in online deals – up 12% from a year back, gauges online surveys.

What can online retailers do to maintain a strategic distance from blackouts and different disturbances? It's an imperative issue on the grounds that an expected one-in-five retailers endured blackouts a year ago. The harm? Forty-five% evaluated they could lose $500,000 to $5 million out of one day because of a site crash.

Gartner experts anticipate a 10% development in the budgetary effect that cybercrime will have on online organizations through current year. They see circulated disavowal of-benefit (DDoS) aggressors exploiting new programming vulnerabilities to start an attack with different sources and frequently various targets. These can be presented through representative possessed gadgets utilized as a part of the work environment and even by means of the Cloud.

Moves to Make Now

While it's likely past the point where it is possible to take significant activities this New Year, Chinese New Year, Ramadan, Diwali, Christmas season, retailers can at present find a way to limit such disturbances. Be that as it may, to truly battle the blackout and downtime challenges, retailers should start making more viable strides after the New Year begins to prepare for the 20xx occasion surge.

Three-of-four online retailers (77%) fortified their online IT guards this year to lessen downtime from a year ago. Downtime unquestionably happens. Considering the regular 99.5% framework uptime, this leaves 43 hours – approximately one-and-a-half days – of downtime yearly.

A key concentration territory ought to be guaranteeing your site can deal with fast and sudden increments sought after. That request can take two structures: wanted request, which ought to be scaled up Cyber Date and undesired request, which ought to be moderated, similar to a cyberattack.

This is what online retailers still can do before the moving toward Big Season..

- Conclude whether you can deal with the expanded movement from wanted request expected amid the Christmas season, particularly on Cyber Date, when online deals take off. You may at present have the capacity to swing to cloud-based administrations to include limit and keep a site crash. In any case, on the off chance that you don't have a cloud supplier, it's likely past the point where it is possible to make those courses of action and exchange your information to the supplier's site.

- Decide in the event that you have sufficient alleviation capacities for DDoS assaults from programmers. The last quarter of the year, principally Christmas season, is when DDoS assaults increment in size and power. In the 20xx final quarter, one DDoS security benefit alleviated assaults that achieved more than 50 gigabits for each second coordinated against web based business customers; the normal assault length was 32.2 hours.

- Discover out how different sorts of DDoS dangers can affect diverse components of your system and decide relief activities that can ensure them, including utilizing a DDoS alleviation benefit.

- Preserve tabs on online journals and web-based social networking destinations since programmers appreciate gloating about their exercises and now and again unveil their next industry target.

- Make beyond any doubt your installment information being gathered stays secure in light of the fact that assailants frequently are following client charge card information.

- For retailers going to start or who have started what's known as the "system solidify," in which no progressions of any sort can be made to their system and framework parts or applications operations until the point that mid-January to abstain from activating downtime, if any serious helplessness that can possibly cause downtime is discovered, a crisis change window ought to be asked for to remediate the issue – notwithstanding amid the "stop." This "stop" hone really is a Payment Card Industry (PCI) direction. In any case, just x% of organizations that store credit and plastic information follow that direction in the middle of their obligatory yearly reviews,

Strategy a New Model for Upcoming Seasonal Opportunity

At the point when the occasion and post-occasion deals surge moderates, start considering the 20xx Christmas season, particularly in case you're truly set on improving your resistances and adaptability against downtime or blackouts and you haven't made significant strides yet. Here are some recommended activities:

- Confer with a counseling firm or a server farm or cloud supplier about what you have to do, particularly, to understand your destinations. Consider really holding a specialist organization that conveys administrations to enable you to scale out and secure your IT operations. Heading off to the cloud doesn't ease your IT duty where security is included. The cloud doesn't really make your applications secure. A specialist organization can work with designers to create and meet these goals.

- Shift to a scale-out IT show so your applications scale out, not up, and this may require application change endeavors to make you application versatile notwithstanding when framework administrations are disturbed in neighborhood districts.

- Act ahead of schedule in the year since this sort of change exertion will require changes over all parts of your framework and application; no genuine alternate way exists and there won't be a great opportunity to roll out these sorts of improvements once the offering season is upon you.

- Embrace cloud-sort stages in case you're an occasional online retailer since they're more unique and it's anything but difficult to scale up rapidly to take care of demand and not bring about additional costs when the request isn't there.

- Look into building up a half and half cloud so those applications that can't be moved to the cloud yet, can keep on being taken care of in their customary way. For example, you may utilize the cloud for web and application levels and keep different operations in your ordinary IT setup until the point when you are prepared to go up against the change actives required to refresh your database condition.

Make sure to test your upgraded framework before the festival season and plan it to help 100% accessibility in light of the fact that your objective must endeavor to dependably be up. This implies securing optional and tertiary offices and assets far separated from your vital office so if a blackout happens in one site, the heap can be naturally moved to a substitute site.

In conclusion, comprehend your key execution pointers, or KPIs – those estimations used to assess the achievement of specific exercises in which you're locked in. To do this well, you should have a firm comprehension of the KPIs over all levels of your applications.

Surely for online retailers, the occasion offering season is basic to their money related quality and even survival. That is the reason it's basic to keep your IT operations up and running and to perceive and repulse digital aggressors.

Be that as it may, recall. You can't do everything. Basically do what you can during the current year and move quickly to plan for the seasonal opportunities

Information Based Driven Strategies to Meet Holiday Shopper Expectations

As indicated by a current report, 46% of purchasers intend to begin their vacation shopping before Nov. 1. Get ready to man your fight stations – the Christmas shopping season is upon us!

To fulfill buyer request and desires this Christmas season, retailers must figure out what the client needs, when they need it, to make it accessible through the channel they need, at the correct minute they need it. As retailers know, while this is basic, it's additionally an activity full of risk because of the many elements and contemplations that come to endure. A year ago for instance, in the basic weeks paving the way to Christmas Day, retailers (particularly clothing) were crashed by various variables, including warm temperatures.

To this end, the undertaking of getting occasion groupings lined up with stock supply and client request can appear to be out and out overpowering. How would I keep away from stock outs and overloads? Shouldn't something be said about managing "shocks, for example, climate and financial conditions and meeting consistently changing purchaser prevailing fashions and patterns that can additionally muddle request guaging and stock allotment?

Considering occasion stock is for the most part secured 9 to a year ahead of time, most of the groupings that will at last be conveyed are as of now arranged, delivered and on their way to the distribution center for downstream assignments. Reordering products and additionally changing print showcasing at this stage is by inconceivable. And keeping in mind that retailers with physical and online stores have the alternative to move stock amongst stores and online channels – it's not a safeguard intends to compensate for arranging and allotment botches, as it can be fantastically expensive.

So what would retailers be able to do at this late date to upgrade marketing portions to line up with shopper request? For one thing, be Practical and move quick. Remember, as every day passes, you lose the adaptability to influence change which can have desperate main concern results.

This is the place progressed investigation sparkles – giving the way to rapidly recognize patterns, openings and occurrences where genuine request is veering from design, to convey basic bits of knowledge important to patch up retail methodologies to benefit as much as possible from the Christmas shopping season.

Progressed investigation gives retailers the ability to comprehend inclines and alter groupings to meet buyer requests just at the last possible second. In the short however basic Christmas shopping season, this gives retailers the capacity to Practically guarantee the Christmas shopping season is a beneficial, gainful and most awesome time.

Here are somewhere in the range of 5 examination driven procedures that retailers can utilize to meet occasion customer desires, and streamline offer through and edges:

Concentrate on Customers that Matter

Concentrate your endeavors on those clients that shop regularly, at the maximum and give the most elevated esteem (versus those that once in a while shop and just purchase freedom stock). Progressed examination demonstrates which client section is purchasing every item class and how frequently they are reacting to advancements. By focusing on showcasing endeavors on these client sections, you can utilize your promoting dollars astutely to seek after your most prominent deals openings and oblige those clients you need to keep on cultivating.

Receiving Distribution Request

Progressed examination, including special cases, for example, those created from "Retail Exception Engines" (stockouts, fast approaching stock outs and overloads), can help retail portions groups figure out what areas require all the more, less or diverse item from the Distribution Center. These measurements can be connected to both block and mortar stores and additionally e-Commerce channels.

Plunge into the Details to Crack the Assortment Code

Progressed examination conveys business insight on genuine/real deals openings and liabilities on an exceedingly granular level. For instance, verifiably a retailer may have high offer through rates on item, yet maybe deals crest just in November, or just in specific stores.

Since deals figures are regularly arrived at the midpoint of over the store armada or potentially channels, sans these granular points of interest, retailers can frequently miss strong chances to move stock and meet client desires. Progressed examination can enable retailers to uncover these chances to appropriately group each store to meet the particular needs and patterns of their client base that can shift by area.

Begin Thinking About Holiday current/not so distant future

An opportunity to begin making arrangements for one year from now's vacation shopping season is when you close this one. Execution is just in the same class as the prep/design. Search for approaches to put the client in the focal point of the arranging procedure; client centricity starts with purchasing, and to this end, the more you can use investigation, the less suspicions you'll be compelled to make, and the more adjusted you'll be with client needs and desires.

To arrange with trust in the number one spot up to one year from now's vacation shopping season, use web based business channels to test styles and hues and utilize these bits of knowledge to extend block and mortar collections in light of item request.

Tangible Information

Not exclusively does the client encounter should be reliable, yet the information you catch on a given client should be spotless and reliably recovered. Information should likewise be entwined over the storehouses of promoting, IT and operations to give a total perspective of the client, and maintain a strategic distance from issues of over-speaking to or under-speaking to client conduct. In the event that a client peruses from one gadget and purchases from another, it could significantly influence your understanding of which encounter is effective. Significant information is important to brands, yet to guarantee the information being gathered is right, trying omnichannel endeavors before the invasion of the occasions is vital.

Retailers need to coordinate the comfort and simplicity of B2B2C leaders, while customizing and putting away information to hold buyers returning and the best way to do that is by making a superior end-to-end client encounter that is driven by client bits of knowledge. Inability to convey on this experience will mean abandoning income that B2B2C leaders will be cheerful to get.

From Big Data to Big Personalization

Utilizing huge information will guarantee that organizations can take in more about purchasers and utilize the data they have through a compelling personalization and division, as indicated by this infographic by Monetate. Believe in Big Data Analytics substitute unstructured business decision will empower you to streamline, analyze and discover real-time market, business, investment, revenue, product, and various form os insights within your transactional data that would have. Do not miss any of the data which related to your business from sales, marketing, customer feedback, vendor feedbacks, social-media, counterfeit and various elemenet which gone unnoticed and magically big data able to predict your future demand or decision and provide answers to all of your major decision. Make your business decision and direction with data accurancy for everything just got pretentious and cleverer.

Is Big Data Big Hype or the Next Big Thing?

A year ago, Big Data appeared to be the trendy expression at each promoting meeting. On the off chance that computerized installment arrangements embraced Big Data, incredible things would happen – to be specific, better focusing of their customers and prospects, and the more prominent capacity to manufacture 1-to-1 connections.

In any case, there likewise appeared to be a Big Disconnect with Big Data. Back in the pre-fall and late-summer, senior substance maker Erin Lynch, composed this article on Big Data being a distinct advantage for advertisers. What's more, I recall how disappointed she was the point at which she was taking a shot at the article. "Nobody needs to speak [with us about Big Data]," she'd say. That is really an embBiggyBoxhment – a few people talked, and gave our group of onlookers some splendid understanding into Big Data. Be that as it may, there were likewise some computerized installment arrangements and advertisers who revealed to us Big Data was be "exclusive data."

Others were reluctant to talk, and revealed to us they thought about Big Data, however didn't feel sufficiently good to discuss it.

So I wasn't shocked not long ago, when SAS and SourceMedia issued a public statement to state most associations presently can't seem to create and actualize a major information methodology. SAS and SourceMedia overviewed 339 information administration experts about their associations' utilization of information administration innovation. The outcomes demonstrate couple of associations exploiting item, client and other information sources.

As indicated by the overview, 21% of respondents don't know enough about Big Data, 15% don;t comprehend the advantages of Big Data, and 9% need information quality in existing frameworks.

So is Big Data the following huge thing, or is it huge buildup?

In principle, Big Data bodes well. In any case, it shows up it will take a long time for Big Data to get on. When advertisers get their hands on Big Data, what do they do with it? In what capacity will advanced installment arrangements utilize it the correct way?

In this article, Dan Darnell, VP of showcasing at Baynote, totals up why retailers may not get a hang of Big Data in 2013.

"Key to this pattern is the idea of calculations and machine learning," Darnell composed. "The enormous information wave is coming, yet couple of organizations will open its energy at any point in the near future."

Will Mobile Payments Soon Reign Supreme?

Shoppers have been reluctant to embrace utilization of portable installment innovation, for example, Apple Pay. As indicated by a Trustev study, just a single in 50 individuals who claim an iPhone 6 are utilizing Apple Pay in a standard premise, in spite of the innovation being available for a year.

One of every five of telephone proprietors had a go at utilizing Apple Pay at any rate once, yet most clients dropped off or just utilize it periodically. In 2014, under 0.5% of all telephones (not restricted to Apple items) fit for making contactless versatile installments were utilized to do as such at any rate once every month.

Monica Eaton-Cardone, COO of question moderation and misfortune counteractive action firm Chargebacks911, noticed that all together for versatile installment innovation appropriation to take off, both the customer and the engineer need to each be as similarly associate in the administration.

Indeed, even Apple has been experiencing issues getting through to buyers, leaving Eaton-Cardone to ask, "If Apple can't do it, who can? What does the wide future for versatile installments resemble?"

"Without computerized installment arrangements energetic about growing new innovation to propel the comfort of versatile installment innovation, buyers won't take after. In any case, without advanced installment arrangements trusting buyers will use the innovation, computerized installment arrangements won't be energetic about growing new innovation," says Eaton-Cardone. "Growing new innovation can be a costly venture. Advanced installment arrangements need to feel positive about customer use in any case. We are not seeing that correct at this point."

Eaton-Cardone is unsurprised that portable installment innovation reception is moderate. While advancements in portable installment innovation can possibly make regular daily existence and installments simpler, numerous purchasers see the innovation as unreliable. In 2014, installment card extortion represented $32 billion in misfortunes in the United States alone, exhibiting a 38% expansion from the $23 billion in misfortunes retailers endured in 2013. The misfortune because of extortion is identical to 0.68% of income. (2)

Unexpectedly, per Eaton-Cardone, Apple is most defenseless against themselves. She calls attention to that with Apple Pay, a fraudster could take a charge card, enter it into a telephone, at that point utilize the telephone to buy Apple items – with no distinguishing proof essential. At that point, when the cardholder goes to debate the fake movement, Apple loses the most.

"At the point when a customer utilizes Apple Pay, they are as yet secured through chargebacks," says Eaton-Cardone. "In any case, chargebacks can be a twofold edged sword, and there is a high probability that those recording deceitful chargebacks will get got."

Eaton-Cardone says that EMV is the best choice for extortion insurance. Until there is a database approving each and every card holder's unique finger impression and computerized personality, EMV is the approach, she bears witness to. EMV depends on a client's previous history to decide whether the buy is substantial or not and furthermore uses a smaller scale chip to store delicate data, as opposed to an attractive stripe.

Through the small scale chip, the client's purchasing examples and ways of managing money are broke down in about a millisecond so as to distinguish suspicious movement. The cardholder should even now confirm the exchange with a PIN number or mark.

EMV has been extensively utilized crosswise over Europe since 2005. The United States is the last created nation to receive the framework; nonetheless, the INTERNATIONAL. installments industry is progressing over into this framework with plans to do as such completely by October 1. Significant organizations, for example, Target, Wal-Mart and Sam's Club have effectively executed the new innovation.

Orders

Deal with every one of your requests, see arrange points of interest, dispatch orders, create solicitations, and so forth.

You can deal with the client arranges in the requests area of BiggyBox Admin Panel.

Seeking and Filter Orders

In the event that there are many requests then you can inquiry and channel requests to process the particular requests.

Request Summary

You can tap on the request to see the synopsis of the request in the correct board.

Operations on Order

Give us now a chance to investigate the activities we can perform on the request outline window.

Check as dispatched

On the off chance that you have handled a request physically through an outsider coordinations supplier, tap on this tab to record the shipment points of interest. You will be required to enter the AWS number and the specialist organization name. An email warning will be sent to the client.

Ship Now

You can utilize this alternative to dispatch the request if a) you are shipping the request utilizing BiggyBox shipping record or b) you have incorporated your own particular delivery account.

Make Fulfillment

Achievements give you better control on satisfying the requests than simply delivering the whole request. You should empower incomplete achievements in the Store Settings to utilize this element. You can make satisfaction for all things or couple of things of the request. You can likewise make solicitations for incomplete achievements.

Scratch off Order

You can scratch off the request by tapping on this tab.

Copy Order

You can copy the request by tapping on this tab.

Create Invoice

You can likewise create the receipt for your request by tapping on this tab.

Print Invoice

You can likewise take a print of your request synopsis by tapping on this tab.

Recover Invoice

You can likewise recover the receipt for your request by tapping on this tab, in the event that you have rolled out improvements in the receipt format.

Resend Order Confirmation

You can resend the request affirmation to the client and additionally the dealer utilizing this summon.

Include Additional Info

You can add extra data to your requests on the off chance that you need to pass such data to your clients after they have put in a request.

View Logs

You can see the historical backdrop of the considerable number of activities you have performed on a request, by tapping on this tab.

Social Media and Messaging Tool (WhatsApp/WeChat/etc..) is a typical Communication Changer for Omni Stream

Digital installment Solutions

At the point when organizations consider which correspondence channel to utilize while drawing in clients; content informing (CONVENTIONAL MSG) is at the highest priority on the rundown. Known as A2P informing, this procedure of associating with purchasers by means of utilization messages is soaring. To that point, 1.7 trillion CONVENTIONAL MSG messages are relied upon to be sent by organizations in 2018, as indicated by Portio Research.

The purposes for this development

Basically, A2P CONVENTIONAL MSG is the omnipresent, savvy, secure, reliable unavoidable and direct channel for organizations to speak with their clients. Furthermore, there is an extensive variety of utilization cases to back that up. Be that as it may, exactly what amount would this be able to correspondence channel enhance multichannel business and relationship hones?

Here are five courses in which A2P CONVENTIONAL MSG benefits the retail and web based business ventures.

It's stickier than email. Not exclusively do somewhere in the range of 7.3 billion individuals send CONVENTIONAL MSG message routinely, yet when clients get messages, they additionally read them rapidly. CONVENTIONAL MSG has an open rate of 99% and 90% of shoppers read a CONVENTIONAL

MSG inside the initial three minutes of receipt, while only 36A% normal open rates for messages.

There is adaptability to achieve one or numerous clients. At the point when your business needs to keep an objective gathering educated or you have to deal with mass movement, one-way informing is accessible. Be that as it may, when you require bi-directional correspondence to make discourse with your objective gathering you can settle on the two-way informing. In the two cases, make a noteworthy battle by utilizing a particular number/ short code or make it novel by utilizing your image name in the message header.

A solid client lifecycle go-to apparatus: Variety of web based business stages and A2P CONVENTIONAL MSG make an interesting collaboration that gives clients the comfort and moment communication. A2P CONVENTIONAL MSG is utilized for approval, confirmation, item data, arrange notice, updates, coupons, vouchers dependability programs.

After a client is snared, it can be a helpful client benefit device. It's an immaculate vehicle when a get back to ask for is fundamental, you need to offer record status data, a client must influence an administration to demand or you need client input.

Amid the operations stage, writings are similarly profitable. CONVENTIONAL MSG offers a straightforward path for setting orders, secret key reset, conveyance refreshes, stock accessibility reports and, obviously, request, installment or shipment affirmation. It's additionally worth specifying that the greater part of this should be possible with the capacity to track, making it simple to know whether clients are getting the message.

The least difficult approach to give benefit notices: A2P CONVENTIONAL MSG is the most streamlined approach to convey benefit subtle elements in the retail/omni-stream world. A buyer arranges an item at the POS and registers with a mobile phone number. At that point a customer gets a content when the item is prepared for get. Straight to the point and no bothers!

Quick, protected and solid. Top-end A2P suppliers can deal with time- and business delicate A2P messages through set up guide associations with portable system administrators. Furthermore, quick conveyance is an immense in addition to because of short inactivity and high throughput rates.

With the retail scene moving at a fast pace, it's basic that organizations in this space have a correspondence channel that can explore those progressions. Regardless of whether it's the universality of content informing or it dependability, security and cost-adequacy, A2P messaging is a strong decision.

Brand Engagement

Similarly as with mindfulness, mark engagement measurements change by channel, and may incorporate paid and non-paid strategies. Concerning mindfulness, I prescribe you isolate paid and non-paid online networking produced mark engagement in revealing, for instance offers of supported and non-paid posts on Facebook.

Cases of brand engagement incorporate Re-Tweets, Facebook Shares, Re-Pins on Pinterest and web-based social networking produced Website visits. It is prescribed you report in view of volumes and cost-efficiencies, to abstain from missing open doors.

At first, I prescribe you institutionalize mark engagement revealing crosswise over channels, by just breaking-out engagement into:

Website visits or

Engagement that builds achieve, for example, offers and re-tweets.

In spite of the fact that a Like may not spur to the degree a Comment would, Re-Tweets and Shares may achieve distinctive quantities of individuals, and brand engagement revealing can get inside and out with "Change Rate," "Intensification" and "Engagement Rate," to begin I've thought that it was best to begin basic.

Exchanges

Like different channels, you need to catch the quantity of requests, deals change, income and the normal request esteem.

The difficulties are precisely writing about web-based social networking impacted online business exchanges, and giving an account of web-based social networking created disconnected deals. (For reasons for outline, I will utilize web based business deals.)

Most Web revealing apparatuses default to announcing deals in light of "last touch," exchanges are credited to the last channel a guest went to before obtaining, which can be fairly deceptive.

An imminent client might be far down the way of influencing a buy when they to visit the last channel, and last touch announcing doesn't consider when the client initially wound up plainly keen on your image/items. Particular to online networking, when providing details regarding deals in light of the "main touch" it is normal to see fundamentally more "impacted" deals than announced with last touch. Following are real outcomes:

> Facebook; 48% expansion in number of revealed orders
> affected by online networking with first touch

> Reddit.com; 86% expansion in number of detailed requests
> affected by online networking with first touch

I prescribe you provide details regarding last touch, and first-touch or another attribution strategy, for a more all encompassing perspective. To have the capacity to think about channels, you ought to do this for all you're showcasing channels.

Expenses

I suggest you isolate costs/announcing for every online networking channel for paid and non-paid showcasing.

You may have coordinate costs, including publicizing, advancements, plan/ improvement and web-based social networking office charges, which might be for a particular channel or should be allotted.

As far as revealing showcasing overheads, most essential is being steady over all advertising channels so you can look at ROI, mindfulness and engagement efficiencies (CPMs). Since a lot of online networking advertising is non-paid, it is imperative to catch and apportion overheads, for instance on the off chance that you have a full-time web-based social networking chief.

Return for Money Invested

Figuring ROI for every web-based social networking channel is income – COGS – coordinate showcasing costs – designated advertising overhead/ add up to channel promoting costs. With exchanges, you ought to ascertain ROI in view of last touch and first touch (or another attribution technique).

Figuring showcasing ROI from late test promoting, what I found was "marked hunts" on Google created the most requests, income and edge… however ROI via web-based networking media channels was ideal.

By having ROI for all channels, my customer will put more assets into online networking, since after some time it might produce more benefit when scaled. He may have missed this open door on the off chance that he just took a gander at volumes.

When investigating ROI, I suggest likewise providing details regarding mindfulness and engagement volumes and efficiencies. Despite the fact that actually not ROI, they are vital to measuring the estimation of online networking advertising.

Truth be told, there are extra online networking benefits not by any means tended to in this article, including huge effect on SEO, verbal, viral advertising and social business.

Figuring the ROI on Your Social Media Marketing

The goals of this article were to enable you to recognize what your online networking channels improve the situation than your other showcasing channels, and to enable you to decide how to designate assets.

With this data you ought to have the capacity to institutionalize give an account of and think about web-based social networking showcasing comes about, distinguish what every online networking channel does best, and better allot assets to enhance general promoting comes about.

This is what I recommend you do next:

> Compile a rundown of your mindfulness and engagement measurements for the channels you utilize
>
> Standardize the measurements as examined above in the Awareness/Engagement areas
>
> Cross-reference the measurements to the merged institutionalize measurements (for instance, re-tweets as "mark engagement expanding reach")
>
> Create reports with lines for every online networking channel (breaking out paid/non-paid), sections for the measurements above, and recipes
>
> Research revealing devices you might need to use for catching mindfulness/engagement comes about.

Senior Corporate Marketing folks has held senior internet business leadership and omni-stream business at retail parts at interesting online stores such as boutique type online store/, Hasbro and content sites Right now counseling, customers incorporate a $600MM+ omni-stream retailer, $200MM+ online business store, $100MM+ DTC omni-stream advertiser and a beginning period internet business store.

The most effective method to Calculate the ROI On Your Social Media Marketing

With most advertisers and advanced installment arrangements having online networking goals, yet not evaluating comes about, there should be a moderately simple approach to provide details regarding web-based social networking showcasing.

The accompanying is not just about giving an account of web-based social networking created mindfulness, engagement, deals and ROI, it's about how to institutionalize and afterward contrast web-based social networking comes about and other promoting channels.

The essential target of this article is to enable you to distinguish what online networking channels improve the situation than your other promoting channels, measure, analyze execution, and enable you to decide how to assign assets.

Mindfulness

Late studies show producing mindfulness is the best online networking promoting objective for generally organizations.

Mindfulness related strategies incorporate paid and non-paid promoting. I prescribe you isolate paid web-based social networking (Facebook show advertisements and supported posts, advanced tweets, advanced pins, and so forth.) and non-paid online networking in detailing.

Cases of mindfulness related strategies incorporate Tweets and Facebook posts. To write about, and look at, I change over online networking mindfulness measurements to Reach (the quantity of individuals conceivably achieved), Impressions (the aggregate number of potential impressions created), Frequency and Estimate-Per-Many Transaction for reach and impressions, which makes conceivable contrasting volumes and cost-efficiencies.

I utilize a rundown of social media measurements, and cross-reference each to reach and impressions, and compute recurrence and CPMs. For instance, Twitter Followers and Facebook Fans = Potential Reach. The quantity of

Twitter Followers times the quantity of Tweets = Potential Impressions. The quantity of Tweets = Occurrence.

Utilizing Feedback to Make a Quality Merchandises

BiggyBox said socialmedia tries to concentrate the criticism on item changes, updates and enhancements. What they are most worried about in current/ not so distant future is giving an awesome item encounter.

"We concentrate on (Net Promoter Score) NPS and keep rates by brand and item class," he said. "What level of things are they keeping when clients are attempting them at home?" Online Store Front enables client to request and attempt on things at home before they choose to buy, returning what they don't need.

Taking a gander at the brand and class gives a standard for desires. For instance, BiggyBox said shorts play out a considerable measure superior to slacks. "That encourages us comprehend whether an item or entire classification is failing to meet expectations," said BiggyBox.

BiggyBox said retailers will extend their product offering in light of client criticism. Notwithstanding, the test is that clients as item trailblazers are working with a constrained edge of reference.

"An individual comprehends what he or she needs or needs, not what is required or needed generally," BiggyBox said. "It's the obligation of the retailer to decide how the expansion will serve clients and friends."

Stocklin said One Click's promoting and client satisfaction groups have shared reports to pass criticism forward and backward, enabling the organization to get items it's missing while at the same time ceasing things that aren't meeting client desires as far as quality.

How Customer Feedback Offers the Best Online Experience

Beside item upgrades, clients likewise give input about the retailer's site, enabling them to audit it and roll out important improvements.

For instance, Online DIY Stores fused a few of the most-requested site highlights to help support shopping productivity and enhance the client encounter.

Among the most widely recognized solicitations from clients was the capacity to get to their record data for speedier checkout and to effectively see arrange history. The site's landing page offers a "My Account" connect that empowers them to spare installment strategies, alter a charging address, see past buys, check charging status, print receipts, track shipments and demand returns or reorders.

"Something we're truly dedicated to is our level of administration," said Online DIY Stores providers in an article for Multichannel Digital installment arrangement. "We tune in to what you need and the 'My Account' highlights were a rehashed ask for from clients."

On the organization's webpage its online truck will refresh without requiring a page invigorate, while a merged checkout page demonstrates the total request with amount, evaluating and sending alternatives.

The inquiry box naturally triggers a dropdown menu of recommended inquiries. Items can likewise be found by entering a section number, which courses clients specifically to the page. These site changes help advance the organization's slogan, "Think that its quick. Get it quick."

Another new element on Online DIY Stores incorporates printer-accommodating item determination sheets. Tables containing measurements, stack qualities and different points of interest are accessible to download in a PDF design, taking into consideration simple reference and sharing.

"Whenever we roll out improvements to our site it is to enhance our client encounter," providers said. "We're proceeding to add new items to address our clients' issues, and are likewise searching for client input for new items to include."

Online DIY Stores keeps on growing its product offering and can find numerous things not promoted on its site. providers urges clients to call an item authority for help with any necessities or inquiries.

BiggyBox said getting criticism from clients in regards to a retailer's site encounter is outstanding amongst other approaches to test convenience. "It distinguishes territories where suggestions to take action aren't generally effortlessly comprehended by end clients, route issues and general usefulness," providers said.

BiggyBox included usefulness issues like broken connections are tended to first. General upgrades are made in the wake of advertising and operations survey the need and general impact.

Will Consumers Survive the Death of Retail?

Branded as of late reported it will be shutting Global. stores. The news takes after International Clothing defaulting on some loans, leaving business, The Limited closing down... This developing rundown of terminations has prompted a huge number of "The Death of Retail" features and web-based social networking posts.

The savage sense of watching something vanish is not just instinctually charming, it likewise gets site hits. I'll concede, I'm blameworthy of this. The feature for this article utilized this snap catching procedure, and, in case you're perusing this sentence, you succumbed to it... once more!

Before long, it can influence you to ponder, would we say we are really seeing the passing of retail? Is it a move to huge box one-stops versus boutique claim to fame stores? Is it only a stage? Is it true that we are on the whole adding to a rubbernecking automobile overload to no end more than a minor collision?

Nobody knows without a doubt, however one can state with conviction that the historical backdrop of web based business, and its advancement to trendy expression mishandled omni-stream, omni channel, multi- gadget, fringe free shopping encounters has been covered with dangerous forecasts.

Instead of getting impeded in a skeptical point of view of everything business, I say quit taking on a similar mindset as an advertiser for a minute and begin adopting the thought process of a buyer. Not only your client, but rather purchasers as a substantial mass of individuals prepared to shop, searching for an arrangement and needing everything at the present time – or possibly with a following day shipping alternative.

The demise ring of the terminations and breakdowns has been concealing the sound of the purchaser's voice. For as far back as couple of years, the purchaser has been the impetus driving everything business, forward. Huge numbers of the battling retailers specified before in this article may have possessed the capacity to fabricate enthralling shopping encounters on the web and in-store, however these developments might not have stayed aware of changing purchaser inclinations and practices.

As advertisers, we regularly go straight for the information when we are terrified and require answers. This can bring about a lot of an attention on execution information and insufficient on customer conduct and the subjective measurements that uncover how shoppers are molding trade patterns.

Finding a harmony between advertising information and buyer bits of knowledge will help you to recognize patterns where the information may point you the correct way, however the customer's voice will truly disclose to you where they need to go.

There are, notwithstanding, two bits of this trade confuse that can help you to take advantage of these turns and turns in customer conduct: client created content (CGC) and email promoting. Presently, I won't plot the majority of the estimations of email and CGC here, however I would like to be clear about the need to discover potential outcomes for incorporating them both in the general examination of your business' execution.

From starting consciousness of your image to long haul dedication, both email and CGC interface with each progression of the client travel. Alongside your quantitative examination, search for minutes when the purchaser purchase when you anticipate that them will use it.

You may find that customers are exceptionally drawn in and dynamic until the point when an item is added to the shopping basket, at that point they level line. In this illustration, take a gander at the last snapshots of engagement and your post-relinquishment advertising endeavors to perceive what's coming up short. Maybe your methodology could profit by a more individual tone or brand voice that addresses the purchaser uniquely in contrast to a motivator that is rehashed in each message.

Furthermore, look to your CGC – appraisals, surveys, group Q&A, client photographs – to check whether your clients are finding better approaches to shop and offer encounters.

For instance, there might be holes in your item page content that could be filled by including your CGC all the more unmistakably. In the event that your item Q&A is loaded with inquiries regarding size, shading, cut and texture, at that point including photographs and recordings put together by past clients could enable these concerned customers to purchase with certainty. Maybe your customers are building ventures with your items that could spur first-time purchasers to genuinely comprehend the estimation of your items.

In the event that each business was fruitful and our industry never showed signs of change, each customer would be cheerful, deals would continually break records and we could all resign early. Tragically, that is simply not how the world functions. As we saw years back with Boundries and Metro Route, and we are seeing now with retailers, for example, PADINI and ASIAN Clothing, there will be startling changes and, at last, customers will get their direction. We simply need to ensure we are listening when they whisper what they need.

Making A More Robust Cart Recovery Strategy

Basic industry measurements demonstrate that over 70% of all web based shopping baskets are relinquished. However retailers for the most part treat all customers who relinquish trucks the same, paying little heed to what things they were looking for. While this one-estimate fits-all approach may work for some, it doesn't work for everybody. The explanations behind forsaking a truck have a tendency to fluctuate in light of truck add up to, and the necessities of the customer additionally tend to change as the cost increments. In this way, utilizing a sweeping methodology for truck recuperation messages is likely costing retailers important deals.

Here's an illustration: I was as of late in the market for a dishwasher and started by shopping on the web. I perused by means of portable PC and cell phone, read audits, trucked (and surrendered) items, and saw items in stores. Amidst my excursion, I began getting deserted truck messages. What emerged to me is that they were not under any condition accommodating. As close as

I was to making a buy, none of these messages persuaded me to do as such. They disappear.

Inability to Launch

These messages disappear on the grounds that they didn't consider the purchaser's inspiration and deterrents to transformation. Somebody looking for a $50 thing likely has diverse requirements and falterings than somebody considering a $800 thing.

Marketing

Showcasing approaches enable you to set up deal, rebate coupons and different exercises for enhanced transformations.

========================

Showcasing approaches enable you to set up deal, rebate coupons and different exercises for enhanced transformations.

How Email and Live Chat Comes intoplay

BiggyBox believes is the default criticism channel for Online Store Front, where the brand gathers the most client data. Online Store Front doesn't do quick input accumulation from email, yet rather lines up the following day with a client. It will likewise email a client after they have finished the attempt on process and have paid for the thing.

BiggyBox believes is an advantageous individual type of correspondence as clients can pick when they read and react to a retailer's message.

"There is a special reward of composed documentation for future inquiries and reactions," she said. "Giving email as an input channel makes it less demanding for individuals to give the data an organization needs to upgrade the client encounter."

Stocklin said that One Click's client joy director sits on a group that additionally incorporates delegates from promoting, innovation, marketing and satisfaction.

The client joy director will total email input he gathers from the majority of the channels and he conveys it to the client group. The group will then choose what activity the brand needs to take in view of the input they get.

Live visit has turned into another way significant way retailers are associating with clients. It gives clients the capacity to make inquiries about an item before they influence a buy or help to influence the checkout to process simpler and accordingly help support deals. It's another input channel utilized by Online Store Front. Getting moment assistance from the contact focus delegate makes the experience a more agreeable one and has expanded purchasing rates.

3 Ways to Convert Email-Obsessed Customers

Because of cell phones, tablets and even brilliant watches, individuals would now be able to get to the web every minute of every day and from anyplace. What are they doing with this time on the web? Incredibly, as indicated by a current report, they're spending an astounding 6.1 hours a day checking their email. Regardless of whether on the tram, at work or in bed, individuals are always in their inboxes.

In any case, that doesn't mean you can simply send your group of onlookers whatever you feel like and anticipate that your messages will perform. Your clients need significant messages at precisely the ideal time—and if your image doesn't finish, they won't waver to hit the erase catch, or more regrettable, withdraw. So in what capacity would marketers be able to want to stay aware of these desires? One awesome technique is to look past the client's inbox first.

It's hard to believe, but it's true: To convey email content that will prompt client transformations, advertisers need to gather data on what clients are doing when they're not checking email. Perhaps they're going by your site, looking at your store, exploring your items et cetera. The information you gather outside the inbox can enable you to convey email that prompts better connections and more deals.

To kick you off, here are three basic moves clients make and how you can follow up on them to send better, more viable email.

Activity 1: An endorser peruses your site

Your reaction: Offer suggestions in view of what they took a gander at

Here's a detail neither web designers nor will advertisers like: More than 95% of first-time site guests won't influence a buy when they to open your site. Try not to give that number a chance to debilitate you, however. Despite the fact that these guests won't not be prepared to purchase right now, they are keen on your image in some way or another.

The key is to benefit from their underlying interest and persistently sustain them so they'll be prepared to purchase some place down the line. Outline an information exchange shape that gets their consideration, and after they agree to accept your email list, send them a robotized welcome note presenting your image. As they keep on browsing your offerings, send messages showing those items and comparable items that may intrigue them. These delicate taps help bump guests closer and nearer to their first buy.

Activity 2: Someone associated with your organization in any capacity

Your reaction: Send a thank you email and offer significant subsequent stages

On the off chance that a client purchases something, send them a thank you email. In the event that a client leaves a survey, send them a thank you email. On the off chance that a client goes to an occasion, send them a thank you email... you get the point. Expressing profound gratitude is a critical piece of supporting your associations with prospects and clients, yet a shocking number of advertisers let this brilliant open door fall by the wayside.

B2B advertisers aren't free, either. While thank you messages are unmistakably profitable for B2C advertising, B2B brands can profit, as well. On the off chance that somebody downloads a bit of your substance, for instance, send an email expressing profound gratitude and offering other supportive substance or item proposals. It's an incredible chance to demonstrate your clients you're tuning in to them and genuinely think about their interests.

Activity 3: Potential clients deserted their shopping baskets

Your reaction: Offer free delivering or a markdown

You know how it goes. You go to a site, glance around and add a few things to your truck. At that point you don't have your credit card ideal beside you or you just get diverted, leaving your truck full without really obtaining anything. We've all done it; all the more particularly, as indicated by BiggyBox Survey, 69 percent of web based shopping baskets are relinquished before the client makes a buy.

Another principle reason potential clients surrender their trucks? Transportation costs. Truth be told, Forrester Research found that 44 percent of individuals who surrender their trucks do it due to high delivering costs. Consequently, an email with a straightforward offer of free transporting might be sufficient to bring the deal to a close.

Powerful truck surrender messages require some extraordinary consideration, particularly tight incorporation between your internet business and email advertising stages. Be that as it may, a focused on, all around created email to these potential clients can profit the two gatherings. The insights bear this out:

- Almost a large portion of the messages coordinated at truck abandoners are opened, and more than 33% of those snaps lead specifically to buys (BusinessCycle).

- People who are focused through relinquished truck messages frequently spend more than what their unique truck add up to was – 55 percent more, by and large (Marketing Leaders).

Maybe the most great detail of all is the straightforward primary concern. As indicated by Salesforce, the normal income for each special email is $0.01, and the normal for an appreciated email is $0.20. The normal relinquished truck email? $5.64.

We may all be living in our inboxes nowadays, however that doesn't mean we don't likewise travel outside them now and then. Focus on your supporters' conduct outside the inbox, follow up on it with focused, significant email informing, and watch your change rates rise more than ever.

The Next Generation of Batch and Blast

Asia-staying Joe likes the brilliant Bermuda shorts and green deck shoes he found on your site. Be that as it may, when he gets the email advancement highlighting the dark winter coat? Not really.

The present customers expect applicable correspondence from retailers, and in this illustration, Joe's desires were not met. It's likewise the sort of case that has been utilized to thump group and-shoot messages as an ineffectual system. In any case, imagine a scenario in which you could even now clump and-impact – and customize.

With division apparatuses, proposal motors, and simple to-utilize lifecycle informing computerization, you can really make clump and-impact messages pertinent to the individual customer. We should investigate how you can utilize these apparatuses to resuscitate your clump and-impact informing.

Division Tools

Devices for division are currently incorporated with most advertising robotization stages and make group of onlookers division less demanding than at any other time. They likewise put the information, for example, web perusing, email and buy movement alongside data gave by the buyer, in the hands of the genuine advertiser, not the IT office. This quick access to information can be utilized to truly improve the general client involvement in an assortment of ways. For example, area information can be utilized to embed nearby store data into messages or target clients in the zone when another store is opening.

Item Recommendations

Once you've assembled division information, you can utilize it to figure out which items to show to the individual client. Utilizing item suggestions in view of supporter information as optional substance in bunch and-impact messages builds the importance of your message, and it should all be possible without building up various varieties of the message. You can utilize them to prescribe comparative items, upsell items, propose frill, or increment normal request an incentive in addition to other things.

Lifecycle Messages

Lifecycle informing robotization is a to a great degree compelling technique for retailers and can be an extraordinary approach to expand bunch and-impact messages. Lifecycle messages, for example, an appreciated arrangement, post-buy arrangement, and shopping basket deserting, are high income drivers, and retailers now can computerize these messages effortlessly. They're as of now extremely significant to your group of onlookers, however you can upgrade the experience for your clients considerably assist with important item suggestions.

Since making one of a kind renditions of everyday messages is never again required, consider investing that spared energy in making more particular informing for these arrangement in view of different elements, for example, wellspring of obtaining or class of items bought. For example, a post-buy arrangement for my new TV ought to be unique in relation to the one for my new earphones. Consolidating this novel informing with suggestions can be a critical win-win.

Having these instruments promptly accessible gives you the capacity to take a one-estimate fits-all email message and make it progressively important. Since that winter coat email to Joe now likewise features the most recent tropical warm-climate things he's certain to l

Wholesale Transaction

Wholesale Transaction permits you simple transfer and import of goods, classifications, clients and requests.

Step by step instructions to Achieve Lucrative Fulfillment

Clients today are always overpowered with data crosswise over a wide range of channels. On account of steady association through computerized innovation change, they're fit for discovering item data whenever, all over the place.

Subsequently, client inspiration for the buying procedure has changed significantly. Clients need the best item (at the best cost), when they need it, and how they need it (purchase in-store, buy on the web, and so forth.). It doesn't take ache for clients to change to an alternate seller in the event that they don't get what they need. While there are a couple of organizations like Apple — where the items are remarkably separated and clients are eager to pay an excellent cost, as well as sit tight for accessibility — this is not the situation for generally organizations.

All the more frequently, organizations endeavor to win clients by going the additional mile to live up to their desires, (for example, paying premium cargo charges to speed up items, and so forth.). How does a venture charm its clients and remain productive in the meantime?

5 Questions to Consider

How about we consider a run of the mill arrange promising and satisfaction process in a business-to-business (B2B) endeavor. B2B organizations can get orders on the web, through deals delegates, interchange transaction exchanges and the sky is the limit from there. Each request is for a particular item and amount. A few requests have an asked for conveyance/deliver date while many don't. Endless supply of the request, the organization must choose how to best satisfy it. For example:

Does it should be satisfied from accessible stock?

Does it should be satisfied from in-travels/planned receipts?

Even however there is accessible stock, does the satisfaction date should be pushed out so it doesn't imperil the satisfaction of future requests from higher need clients?

Does it bode well to satisfy the request from an optional satisfaction area, which will bring about an extra cargo charge?

If the client arrange requires fabricating and there is a lack of parts, does it bode well to assist parts (and cause extra charges) to satisfy the request on time?

As far as we can tell, most organizations don't have an organized and fundamental system to answer these inquiries. Without this, they regularly fall back on a first-start things out served satisfaction arrangement, which is an imperfect method for taking care of the request preparing and satisfaction process.

What are a portion of the issues with the first-start things out served display? In the first place, you might be allotting accessible supply to bring down need clients, abandoning you without enough supply to satisfy future requests from high-need clients. Second, you might be satisfying a request with a future due date utilizing current stock. Thusly, you hazard not having enough stock to satisfy future requests that come in later with that day dispatch ask.

Given these variables, what is an ideal request satisfaction procedure to send in your association? Since we are not living in a universe of unbounded supply, this is a vital inquiry for each venture to consider, as the repercussions can be huge. At whatever point a venture doesn't satisfy a client arrange on time, its administration levels are contrarily affected, income lost and client steadfastness is conceivably dissolved.

Then again, if the organization goes well beyond to satisfy orders (bringing about speed up charges all the while), its productivity is contrarily affected. When contriving an organized and precise request satisfaction procedure, an organization must assess these exchange offs to decide the most ideal approach to satisfy orders.

Online Store Front

Deal with your webpage content, which incorporates subjects, pennants and slides, route, websites, static pages, payment solutions, structures and records.

Online Store Front

It is essential to have a dynamic, delightful and outwardly appealing store to catch your client's consideration. When you have your store facilitated on the BiggyBox stage, you have the freedom to outline the look and feel of your store through your BiggyBox administrator.

Site segment contains following subsections:

Slides

Slides are pictures that can be utilized as a part of a gathering. The most widely recognized utilize is to utilize slides as a component of merry go rounds on your landing page. At the point when a client visits your store, these slides appear consistently. Critical declarations identified with your store and other limited time exercises can be shown by means of Slides.

Route

Route enables you to characterize route menus for your customer facing facade.

Flags

Flags are static pictures for your store. You can utilize standards to indicate limited time offers, feature highlighted item/class or for subsidiary connections.

Sliders, Banners and Navigation, can likewise be a piece of topics however keeping them here enables you to utilize similar pictures or route over different subjects without expecting to reproduce them.

Static Pages

You can include website pages for your store in Static Pages area. The pages could be instructive like 'About Us', 'Merchandise exchange' or could be points of arrival for your showcasing efforts. BiggyBox permits the production of dynamic website pages which can incorporate subject gadgets or structures.

In BiggyBox, we don't confine you to static HTML5 content for pages however you can make dynamic formats similarly you create subject pages. The capacity to incorporate topic gadgets or structures in your pages opens up a plenty of potential outcomes.

Web RSS's

Web journals are exceptionally compelling instruments of showcasing, declarations, client engagement and SEO. BiggyBox offers complete inherent blog usefulness for your store that empowers you to run and advance proficient online journals in your store.

Blog Entries

Blog Entries are posts or articles in a specific blog that are appeared backward sequential request on the blog page. You can oversee blog entries for various websites in this segment.

Records

Records segment enables you to transfer documents that can be referenced on the store which incorporates however is not restricted to the item portrayal, blog page, static page, classification page and so on. The documents can likewise be referenced in CSV records utilized for mass import of items.

Subjects

Subjects area enables you to deal with the topics for your store. BiggyBox enables you to import numerous subjects. You can likewise indicate diverse topics in light of client's gadget or different conditions.

Structures

BiggyBox has an effective Form era ability. You can redo all the current structures e.g. enlistment, shipping address, enquiry shapes utilized as a part of store topics or can likewise characterize custom structures.

Index: An Engaging Sales Driver

The State of Catalog Marketing in the Digital Era

While the index is as yet a critical piece of a retailer's promoting endeavors, a large number of them are proceeding to move dollars and center to computerized endeavors, as they likewise overhaul their inventory methodology in another time. It's just plain obvious, which significant retailers are making the move from the conventional inventory and executing an advanced system.

Around twenty years back, I delighted in the simplicity with which I could take a gander at an inventory and choose in a glimmer whether it was deserving of adulation or manhandle.

In that vintage twentieth-century time, I could put forth a defense just from getting what was in the letter drop and slipping on a couple of glasses.

And still, at the end of the day, subliminally I knew I was living before. Online lists were thundering, and some printed lists were dumping custom for the New Age.

Here we are, on the cusp of Anno Domini current/not so distant future, and any of us who assert an impartial and definitive examination of the inventory showcase – particularly "duplicate," which gets or repulses reaction – would be advised to permit at any rate identicalness to e-indexes or be uncovered as fuddy-duddies..

Identicalness is (at any rate) all together. A few inventories have essentially included an online adaptation with few or no wording changes. Others tailor their duplicate to the medium. But others have surrendered printed forms by and large, expecting that anybody in a position to rate their wording will likewise be web crawlers.

That is the place we are. Quite a while from now? Hello, ask me in five years, expecting we both are as yet alive and still in business. Until further notice, expect the medium isn't the message. We're taking a gander at duplicate, and that exists as a solitary factor, regardless of whether on paper or on the screen.

Two disclaimers

Before going along with me in what might be a suicide mission, consider two factors that can influence each of our responses, decidedly or contrarily:

To start with, neither I nor anybody sees each inventory. We're restricted to those that cross our work areas in printed shape or show up on our screens in computerized frame.

Second, duplicate that interests to one peruser may shock another. We're managing in general terms here. That this section has survived every one of these years is an accomplishment that may survive or may go into history. –

Imagine a two-page spread of armless upholstered seats. No foundation, just limbo. Would you be able to fabricate fervor or expectation without including a heap of odds and ends that may reduce more than draw in?

Here's the "plug" heading:

Beat and blues:. Swoops and bends stream like ikat to paisley, menswear to bohemian, tufted velvet to nail-heads, have seat to visitor seat.

Each word tallies. Each seat has its own particular modified portrayal and every depiction bids without dismissing the past or next seat in line. Simply the start of one:

Sasha Dining Chair Striking Silhouette with an exquisite, secured cushioned back and rich tight seat is keenly custom fitted in a dynamic, ikat-enlivened example...

Best No. 2: Coldwater Creek

Here's an inventory that never disappoints the peruser. One imagines the marketing specialist resolved to expand a business commendable picture. Every portrayal some way or another incorporates a remarkable offering recommendation. Maybe a couple can coordinate the unerring mix of visual interest and specialized interest. Illustration, simply the start of the depiction of a gathering of shirts:

Simple Care Long Sleeve Shirts

Completely the most flexible fundamentals in your closet – with practically no pressing required. You'll quickly see how we've quietly refreshed customary fitting points of interest to supplement your style today – in addition to we've picked an unbelievable elite cotton that opposes wrinkles like a champ...

The Company Store

Astounded that this veteran advertiser, in its 100th year, is snatching consideration at a pace past such a large number of that modernized their depictions? The Company Store is an evergreen. You say "slug" duplicate is out of design? Ideal on, for a list settled in a letter box. However, online – on the off chance that you need to contend, you snatch and you shake ... leaving space for proficient content.

Economy of words infrequently reverse discharges. Not here. For instance, take note of the snugness that drives affect for window boards. To start with sentence of the content:

Greenery Leaf and Solid Linen Window Panels

Vaporous and light (yet sufficiently considerable for security), our unadulterated cloth boards are a representation of loose refinement, upgrading your perspectives with exquisite examples and common surface.

The web form endures here, and if that were the main medium, this advertiser would have missed the watercraft. Here's web duplicate for the indistinguishable thing:

Invigorate your space in a moment. These window boards include the blustery, daintily finished complete that makes cloth an enduring top choice. In a variety of common and sherbert shades, this flexible window ornament board has a place in any style, from exquisite to easygoing. Do you detect levelness supplanting tune? Regardless of the possibility that you don't, the web variant merits a "Huh?" sherbert? That by itself is sufficient for those whose corporate pride has been injured to sue ... notwithstanding out and out separation in any event for isolated upkeep.

Best No. 4: Catalog Classics

Who might expect index depictions that interweave motivations to purchase with certainty verging on a comical inclination?

Threat sneaks there, yet in these skilled hands the peruser is lifted back to those more settled, gentler circumstances in which he or she really read the depictions instead of just angled through for a conceivably needed thing.

A case, on the back cover, is a couple of shoes estimated at $79.95. (The whole list is a return, since costs all through still end in 95 pennies as opposed to the present standard substitution, 99 pennies.) Total duplicate:

TORTUGA SANDAL

Totally hip and totally dazzling, these colored and hand-painted cowhide shoes have a boho vibe and no-heel comfort. Velcro-close instep band keeps them safely on your feet; comfort footbed and no-slip bottoms. Imported. Entire sizes 6-10. Indicate Turquoise Blue or Red.

This practically influenced the Top Four: To unwind the Back

The index's title alone creates the coveted reaction – I need one."

The main reason this inventory isn't on the highest level is its substitution of speculations where specifics may make a superior showing with regards to of snatching and shaking. Case, subhead in a full-page depiction headed "The ULTIMATE EXECUTIVE CHAIR":

Finally a seat that fits and is agreeable. All influenced conceivable via watchful consideration and client to benefit. Best seat I at any point had.

They didn't require a marketing specialist for this, in light of the fact that no particular helper has been transmitted. It's "Rah! Rah!" without "Here's the reason."

"Most noticeably awful?" Only on a near level

In the event that this yearly investigation didn't exist, neither would "most exceedingly bad." But down here in Copywriter Purgatory we review on the "bend," and oversights that harm reaction drag down the similar position on any catalog

Here is a checklist of B2C ecommerce features that can be used for effective B2B operations:

Pricing

> Create unlimited price lists and control which of your customers have access to which price lists.

> Recognize past orders and use that information again, such as order quantities and credit limits.

> Control personalized products and shipping prices for individual customers.

Account Management (Customer Side)

> The ability for customers to view previous orders, including order status and line items

> Edit, view and analyze back order items.

One main account for customers with the ability to assign sub accounts for individuals within the company

The ability to display "request service call"

Request an email when items are back in stock

Offer a quick order system to use product codes for ordering

Provide the recommended retail price and trade price in all areas of the site

View saved and abandoned orders to better target customers and what they are interested in

Promotions

Target specific customers with personalized promotions and special offers

Create special incentives to refer a friend or meet some other requirement.

Manage bundle promotions.

Offer tiered discounts for specific customers.

Remove promotions after they have been used a set number of times.

Product

Integrate with a third-party warehouse to sync stock levels immediately.

Set certain products to appear in a set template.

View related products.

Content Management

Display different templates to specified groups of customers.

Display product videos and pictures in several different sizes.

Display in-depth product attributes and comparison charts.

Multisite Management

An agile website that displays on a single centralized platform in multiple SBU windows (B2B, B2C, forums, blogs, microsites, etc.)

Order Management and Checkout

Add mass items to the shopping cart with one click.

Offer a "repeat order tab" to duplicate a past or saved order.

Accept multiple payments for the same order.

Ship to multiple addresses in the same order.

Other Features

Fast search options to find items from different suppliers through a custom search (by country, location, etc.).

Price and feature comparisons for all brands within a SKU.

Process orders automatically after a set period of time with credit limits.

Auto-generate email to remind users to repeat orders.

Auto-detect customer location with GEO IP and automatically display the correct storefront for the location

Omni-Stream Integration

With any real programming usage, you are changing the whole operation of the organization and everybody's obligations. What's more, if it's not done accurately, you can make exorbitant disturbances to your business, and additionally have significant spending overwhelms and longer-than-arranged usage. Worldwide IT thinks about demonstrate that half of all real IT anticipates are not executed on time or inside spending plan.

7 Steps to Successful Systems Implementation

Expecting you have made an intensive frameworks determination showing with regards to and have obtained the correct framework for your online business or direct-to-client business, you now need to delineate the basic issues for a usage. Giving careful consideration to these 7 components will help make your task a win.

On the accompanying pages, I present to you the 7 stages you have to take for fruitful frameworks usage.

Undertaking administration

Changes to new frameworks regularly get off track since organizations neglect to design the task practically or they don't execute or deal with the venture by the arrangement. Keep in mind that real frameworks transformations are not simply IT anticipates. Organizations ought to keep up joint obligation with the merchant in the venture arranging process, upkeep of the task design status, and in addition some level of control over the usage.

All key client divisions and partners ought to have portrayal on the undertaking group, including the call focus, site, satisfaction, administration, promoting, stock control, advertising and back. Colleagues should share obligations regarding change, preparing and effective culmination of the venture undertakings.

The product merchant ought to have a period tried venture technique and give an abnormal state general arrangement. As the advanced installment arrangement customer, your occupation is to build up the point by point design with the merchant, moved down with detail errands and appraisals.

For instance, a summed up plan may have a rundown of framework alterations, yet do not have the points of interest that should be ordered. These may incorporate research, determinations, sign-offs, program specs, programming, testing and close down, and the different levels of testing and program coordination once more into the base framework.

Plan for possibilities, and attempt to keep interruptions to the business to a base. We have seen frameworks run live with administration at first unfit to get their most every now and again utilized reports — this can be a major issue.

Similarly, you should plan the go-live for the slowest time of the year. In shopper retail and web based business organizations, frameworks by and large aren't brought live from September through Jan. 15.

The frameworks undertaking ought to have a senior director who goes about as the task support. The undertaking ought to be checked on intermittently by the controlling board of trustees to keep tabs on its development. This guarantees senior administration on down to the division directors are focused on progress.

When you have an arrangement that bodes well, ensure you oversee by the arrangement. This sounds basic, however many organizations and merchants unearth it.

Ahead of schedule in the venture distribute an every other week status report. When you get inside a couple of months, you might need to have week by week telephone call gatherings and notices. Inside 30 days of go live, hold day by day gatherings and rundown what should be accomplished.

Process change and best-hone usage

Numerous web based business and DTC organizations neglect to address process and strategy changes that could capitalize on the new framework speedier. This implies they are less well-suited to pick up the coveted proficiency from the transformation.

So you may need to reexamine how the procedures and frameworks that encompass the robotized frameworks need to change as the new framework is introduced.

These procedure changes will differ with the sorts of frameworks. With a distribution center administration framework (WMS), for instance, these procedure changes may incorporate seller consistence, announcing of receipts, executing new strategies for picking, stock cycle tallying techniques et cetera.

A request administration framework (OMS), then again, will have an alternate way to deal with overhauling the client, administration announcing, interface and support of web clients, adjusting and interfaces amongst OMS and bookkeeping, discount and credit forms between client administration, and returns preparing.

What existing techniques and frameworks would you be able to strip away to include effectiveness? What new procedures and systems are required or attractive? What best practices ought to be considered and actualized? These are similarly as imperative as a fruitful execution of the new framework.

Framework parameter designs versus alterations

A standout amongst the most predominant missteps that organizations make in actualizing frameworks is endeavoring to recreate their current frameworks. Changes increment cost, prolong the execution time allotment and increment chance. We've seen organizations demand alterations just to acknowledge in the principal year of operation that there were better methods for utilizing the new framework than endeavoring to reproduce the old.

Most frameworks available can be designed utilizing parameter switches that set choices and give an alternate identity to the application, enabling it to be executed in various sorts of organizations. This permits modifying an application without adjustments; saying this doesn't imply that you won't at times need or need a few alterations.

Numerous applications have hundreds to more than 1,000 framework control switches. The merchant will, clearly, need to prepare your staff on the framework and enable you to do judicious switch settings.

This is detail work that frequently takes half a month of thought. It's imperative to comprehend the outcomes of how a switch is set, at that point test, and after that change the switch setting if vital and rehash testing.

Fruitful document transformations

There are 200 to 500 tables and documents in a full-work OMS, so you have to permit enough time for record transformations.

The larger worries for fruitful document change include:

> Deciding what documents ought to be changed over by means of programming versus building tables and documents physically. You can't for the most part bear to program change over many records, however you should change over your client, thing and request documents. What exertion is included and at what taken a toll?

> Who will assemble the many different tables and records required for the new framework and how? These incorporate distribution center canister area pattern; merchant record and related buy orders; rainchecks; offer and source code documents; dispatching and preparing tables; diagram of records, et cetera.

> Another approach to take a gander at these exercises is that early prologue to the required records and usefulness begins laying the basis for techniques and obligations that are required by the task group.

> What history would it be a good idea for you to change over? At first organizations need a long time of history, yet what is practical and at what taken a toll?

> During the transformation, survey the nature of the change as far as the quantity of records and the exactness of the information changed over. Invest adequate energy to determine, program and test the transformation programs.

Consider your arrangement for slicing over to new framework and document change of the latest records and databases. In what capacity will you deal with this so your records and databases on the new framework are present at the go-live time? What amount of time will be required to change over records?

For bigger organizations, will there be slipped by time to make the transformations from the most recent day on the old framework and raise the new framework?

Various occurrences of the product and database

You will require various occurrences or duplicates of the product/database and application. Most programming contracts confine you to utilizing just a single duplicate of the framework and one reinforcement for recuperation without consulting for numerous set utilize. There are extra permit charges for the extra duplicates that are frequently neglected in the agreement transactions.

You ought to have no less than two duplicates or segments for applications: one for improvement and preparing, and one for creation. Bigger organizations may require three duplicates. The benefit of this is you can secure creation to keep clients from accidentally altering or obliterating generation documents.

Programming preparing and strategies

Likely the most under-arranged zone is in preparing and composing methodology. You have to comprehend that the seller will give documentation just about the application and, best case scenario, how the framework works as far as usefulness.

The merchant's approach is regularly to "prepare your coach." From there, it's your duty to create preparing materials and methodologies for the different divisions and the new strategy and standard working strategies (SOPs) that are required.

Most organizations don't have full-time mentors. It's a smart thought to prepare every division director on the application, and afterward have them build up the SOPs and set preparing for their specialty. The greater part of this should be institutionalized with the goal that the documentation is at a similar level of detail over the operational offices.

It by and large takes 6 a year after usage for organizations to begin feeling great with the new frameworks. It might take more time to accomplish the ROI from the application. Preparing is the absolute most critical thing you can do to abbreviate the expectation to absorb information.

Most merchants offer the underlying preparing, as well as further developed direction for super clients. Financial plan for the extra preparing; it's the littlest piece of the aggregate cost.

What's more, play out a post usage review 30 to 60 days after the go-live. Recognize the people and divisions for which extra preparing is fundamental.

Careful testing

Everything must be altogether tried — frameworks parameters, changes, transformation programs. Testing implies having sufficient energy and the inclusion of the clients, and after that contrasting test comes about with expected results.

Outstanding amongst other approaches to make sure that the framework is prepared for execution is to lead a gathering room pilot. This includes running all the application capacities with a blueprint of the framework.

Run every one of the procedures from start to finish. Utilize scripted test information for each kind of capacity. Test the interfaces to different frameworks. Get and process site exchanges to the business framework.

Are all the warehousing capacities operational? Run and print the key reports. The undertaking group should run the meeting room pilot.

This will take some arranging and coordination, however it's the most ideal approach to decide whether the framework has been designed effectively; if adjustments are modified and tried accurately; and how the new records, tables and databases will show up with your information. It's likewise a sign of whether the framework is really prepared for execution.

As you reveal mistakes, issues and different shocks, backpedal and rerun the usefulness with the redressed projects and contrast the outcomes with expected results.

In the event that you have built up your preparation strategies and SOPs, this is an incredible opportunity to perceive how compelling they are and how they should be tweaked.

Firmly following these 7 stages will enable you to guarantee a fruitful frameworks Implementation, which will pay profits for a considerable length of time to come.

Promoting in Multiple Sales Channels

A standout amongst the most complex assignments in multichannel offering is getting ready item substance to help numerous business channels. While you need some consistency between how items are spoken to in your physical store, your site and on B2B2C leaders, the way your items are spoken to differs generally. For instance, an item depiction on a rack tag in your store wouldn't persuade an online customer to purchase a similar item on your site.

B2B2C leaders, then again, may as of now have all the substance they require on your product things, they simply require your stock information. So keeping in mind the end goal to amplify deals in the greater part of your channels, yet keep up a reliable brand involvement, it is imperative for multichannel advanced installment answers for comprehend the most ideal approaches to create channel-particular substance.

The Varying Roles of Product Data

Item information is a key segment of successfully conveying your image cross-channel. Be that as it may, before you start to circulate that information, it is imperative to first see how thing information ought to be utilized as a part of each channel and how it impacts deals. For instance, in-store clients utilize the data exhibited on the physical bundle to settle on a buy choice while the SKU exists essentially to enable advanced installment answers for oversee checkout. On the web, the item SKU is a basic part of classifying stock for computerized installment arrangements, however the client depends on quality portrayals to settle on a buy choice. In B2B, deals reps depend on the thing information inside the list to viably offer and keep up the respectability of the brand and item.

While it's to some degree natural to see how each channel utilizes item content, dealing with the information is far less instinctive. When moving toward this issue the key idea to get a handle on is that albeit each channel requires an alternate portrayal of the item information, the center item information is the same. So how would you keep up center item information in a solitary area yet exhibit item information in a way that boosts deals in every deal channel? Most multichannel merchant s we converse with say this is by a long shot the most tedious and costly assignment in their multichannel condition.

Synchronization is Not the Answer

While trying to share information over various channels, many organizations match up item data between frameworks, which at that point push the substance to every deal channel. Ace Data Management (ADM) is a typical device used to execute this system, yet I'm not persuaded ADM is not the correct approach for item data administration since it depends on synchronization. Consider this – ADM is an extraordinary decision for overseeing client or provider information since it refreshes a solitary occurrence of that information over all areas to guarantee the data is predictable crosswise over channels. For instance, if a computerized installment arrangement discovers the client has another telephone number, the client record is overwritten with the new number so any individual who gets to that record has the latest data.

Item information doesn't work a similar way. Item information should be a superset of EVERY channel's prerequisites. So ADM won't work in this situation since it enables representatives to overwrite another's thing refresh.

Accordingly, nobody possesses the information and everybody claims the information. Multichannel items require an establishment of item information for each SKU that speaks to the "brilliant thing," which is a superset of all data accessible about that thing, notwithstanding a different perspective of that item accessible for every deal channel containing just the information guides required toward drive deals and work that channel productively.

Where Do You Store Product Data?

An advanced installment arrangement's item information can start
from better places. It can originate from the computerized installment
arrangement's own item depictions or from various providers. The test is
that item information from various frameworks is regularly in numerous
configurations. To accommodate these distinctions, item information should
first be standardized. Once standardized, at that point it can be expended in
each channel.

Numerous computerized installment arrangements look to their eCommerce
stage to combine their item data in light of the fact that eCommerce item
portrayals have the most extraordinary information necessities. In any case,
this isn't the correct decision. Online business stages don't have the essential
apparatuses to control item information (think mass alters or information
transformations) or stock it to different channels. These stages weren't worked
for that reason.

Rather, advanced installment arrangements require a concentrated area to
store the parent SKU and every cycle of an indistinguishable item from it
would show up in each channel. This sort of framework enables item data to
be kept up and improved by channel.

An item substance or data administration framework (terms frequently
utilized conversely) is an extraordinary answer for multichannel merchant
s. A data administration can source information from various spots, paying
little heed to design at that point empower computerized installment answers
for standardize the information and make that "brilliant" thing from which
they can control and syndicate item information to an assortment of offers
channels, as each channel requires. Taking control of your item information
can enable you to enhance operations, boost deals and can be a playbook for
making capable cross-channel content on the web and disconnected for both
your B2C and B2B clients.

Must-Try Channels for Building Customer Loyalty

Client unwaveringness is the way to a business' prosperity. While procurement is likewise vital, your center clients are the ones who will get the income and work as

It's additionally a financially shrewd business system to concentrate consideration on enhancing client steadfastness. That is on the grounds that it costs as much as 6-7 fold the amount of to secure another customer than it does to hold a present one. That as well as steadfast clients spend more than new clients.

So how might you best achieve your dedicated supporters and ensure they're dealt with? Here are some showcasing channels you should attempt that will help support client devotion:

Mobile Search

Portable quests are outperforming desktop seeks but numerous advertisers neglect to put resources into a positive versatile UX for their clients. When you consider that just about two out of at regular intervals spent online is on a cell phone, that is a major error.

Most importantly if your site is not versatile amicable, you will lose some of your clients. A poor versatile site lessens a client's trust in the brand and makes them more averse to buy from that brand.

Truth be told, 79% of customers who had a negative site encounter are probably not going to come back to that site once more. It likewise impacts deals amid a buy. A deferral of two seconds of stacking time amid a buy exchange prompted as high as 87% relinquishment rates.

What to do? Ensure your site is quick stacking and portable amicable with natural site menus and simple to-get to buy data and streamlined checkout forms.

Messanging

Conventional Msg such as SMS devotion programs are an extraordinary approach to connect with your center clients: 48% of buyers said that

Conventional Msg is their favored methods for accepting dedication program messages.

Ensure you treat your Conventional MSG clients with elite specials and valued customer offers. This gives your customers the motivating force to join and to remain. The best thing is that the clients who agree to accept Conventional Msg reliability programs need you to market to them.

Messaging is anything but difficult to-use to the advertiser and helpful to the purchaser. Sending customized and focused on offers in light of client inclinations and buying history can bring about higher ROIs and changes.

Latest Messanging Tool Is Whatsapp

WhatsApp Marketing characteristics:

A professional and effective platform to communicate with potential customers or create a loyalty program.

Your bulk whatsapp messages along with images or videos and unlimited characters.

A video or picture is worth than thousand words. Enrich your bulk whatsapp messages attaching a photo, video or vcards.

Create and upload lists of potential clients with mobile phones. Database lists are stored in your user panel to send bulk whatsapp messages at any time.

Enjoy bulk whatsapp service via WhatsApp media with more than 1,000 characters per message. Which is more than enough to communicate effectively, and with the possibility to attach images, vcards or videos. A Viral Youtube video URL inside a Vcard to generate thousands of views.

We guarantee the delivery of your campaigns thru our platform to your contact lists/databases. You will also receive a stadistics report with deliver, read and not read messages. We have the ability to generate an automatic free reply when potential users answer your bulk WhatsApp campaign.

WhatsappMarketing does not sell or buy databases, as we fulfill the data protection clause at our Privacy Policy to make sure your databases are secure and safe.

Our bulk whatsapp platform could be use into mobiles, tablets and PC.

Marketing Booths

Now and then it's critical for online stores to get their apparatus and get disconnected for some time. Having individual client contact where you can cooperate, answer addresses and enable clients to test-drive your item can be an essential approach to produce new enthusiasm for your image and to strengthen existing associations with steadfast clients. Ensure the staff is very much educated and friendly and that your show draws consideration for a triumphant occasion.

Social Media

Web-based social networking ought not be disparaged with regards to directing people to sites. Studies demonstrate that more clients discover sites due to online networking than on account of web seeks.

In any case, online networking doesn't just bring you clients. At the point when utilized right, online networking enables clients to remain drew in with their favored brands.

Some online networking advertising tips:

> Spread the word by putting resources into boosting well known posts suggested by site chiefs.

> Share photographs and recordings.

> Respond rapidly to client benefit questions.

> Content Marketing

In the realm of YouTube and Instagram, it's anything but difficult to overlook how critical substance is to customers. Without a doubt, an ostentatious picture will snatch the client's consideration, yet offering all around inquired about substance that spotlights on the client and how your item can profit them is the delegated gem of showcasing.

Indeed, pioneers of substance showcasing produce about 8 times more site movement than non-pioneers. Unique substance composed by learned journalists can possibly soar your image's believability, review and transformation rates (six times higher than the individuals who don't embrace a substance promoting system).

Live Chat

Giving your customers the capacity to visit with a client benefit agent and make inquiries about your item or administration before making a buy or amid the checkout procedure can help support deals. Live visit helps the clients who are on your site (i.e. intrigued and prepared to purchase) to settle on obtaining choices. Getting moment encourage is helpful to the customer and organizations who have embraced it have seen purchasing rates increment.

Email

It's a blast from the past. While new mechanical promoting stages are developing in notoriety, email is a long way from dead: 80% of INTERNATIONAL. retailers say that email drives client maintenance.

Inviting clients, sending rewards, tips, advancements and customized email messages, all work to keep up faithful clients. 88% of clients who got birthday messages from an organization said it upgraded their image devotion. Experiment with these channels to build client maintenance for your business and offer your involvement with us!

Versatile Marketing Best Practices: Targeting Brick-and-Mortar Shoppers

Around eight out of 10 customers utilize their cell phones while shopping in-store, as indicated by inquire about from Google. They could be contrasting costs, looking into item data, perusing surveys, or notwithstanding investigating your rivals.

Propelled portable focusing on innovation enables you to "unique mark" individuals who have gone by your area; and that opens up a universe of conceivable outcomes. It empowers you to adopt a one of a kind strategy to speaking with those prospects later on, and it helps your capacity to advance rehash store visits and buys, activity to your online business stage, mark dedication and evangelism, or, if that individual left your store undecided, a first-time deal.

Individuals who have gone to your physical area speak to a particular and significant prospect gathering. Here's the manner by which you can utilize versatile to provoke them to make a move.

The energy of cross-gadget retargeting

Cross-gadget innovation recognizes a client over his or her numerous gadgets through either probabilistic or deterministic coordinating. The last uses checked variables to recognize clients, for example, email delivers they use to sign in crosswise over gadgets. Probabilistic coordinating depends on calculations to dissect a blend of mysterious information focuses, for example, area, time of day, gadget sort, program, IP address and that's just the beginning, to make educated suppositions about clients' personalities.

When you have recognized somebody who has gone to your store, you can retarget them not simply on their portable, but rather on different gadgets, as well. For ideal outcomes, pick a message most appropriate for the season of day, channel and the potential beneficiaries' perspective. For instance, you might need to serve a versatile show promotion with a promo code whenever they are close to your store, though a video advertisement with the most recent on your spring accumulation may work best on their desktop, at night, when they are more open to that sort of top to bottom correspondence.

Alternately, you can likewise utilize cross-gadget retargeting to recognize individuals who have gone to your site, and afterward serve them versatile promotions when they are close to your physical area. On the off chance that you are having accomplishment with site-based retargeting efforts, you can utilize portable promoting to extend those projects by taking advantage of an extra area based group of onlookers.

Try not to Lose Your Customer Because Your Retargeting is Bad

Retargeting is an awesome approach to remain best of your client's brain. Ideally you're retargeting endeavors will get your client to snap and come back to your site, and make that buy.

However, awful retargeting limits the relationship you have with your client. Envision being a blocks and-mortar retailer and running outside in light of the fact that you see somebody in the city who was in your store taking a gander at streak drives, and instructing him to return since despite everything you have them in stock.

At that point envision taking that client by the hand, driving him to those blaze drives, and the client saying they aren't the size he needs. Or, on the other hand more terrible, you take him back to the store, and you don't have the glimmer drives that you disclosed to him despite everything you had in stock.

Humiliating? Indeed. A major issue? Possibly. And keeping in mind that it's not likely a blocks and-mortar case like the above situation, it is something that happens very much of the time in the web based business world.

How about we utilize Lids for instance. I'm an incessant Lids customer. I purchase a great deal of leeway things from them. Through my buy history, Lids knows I purchase measure L and XL shirts, and size S or S/M caps. Tops likewise knows I sometimes purchase New York Giants and New York Yankees attire for my child, since I additionally look for kids' sizes.

In any case, Lids' retargeting does not mirror my purchasing inclinations. Here's a case of an advertisement that appeared on GoComics.com toward the beginning of today:

I browsed Lids and had already taken a gander at the majority of the things (or comparative things) in this specific standard, and beforehand got one thing in a Lids store, so the promotion piqueed my advantage.

Be that as it may, as should be obvious here, two things I tapped on in the Lids advertisement were out of stock, and a third was just accessible in a size S – which is my cap measure, however a long way from being my shirt estimate:

So what can Lids – and an incalculable number of other omnichannel computerized installment arrangements – do to guarantee its retargeting endeavors and spending plan doesn't go to squander?

Make beyond any doubt your stock administration framework is talking with your partner showcasing program. On the off chance that those two universes are adjusted as one, these false-trust client situations won't happen.

Set practical security levels to guarantee that regardless of the possibility that a thing you're retargeting is out of stock in your circulation focuses, it's not erroneously observed as a thing that is as yet accessible to be sent from store.

Add your client's inclinations and shopping history as a layer to your subsidiary promotion program. This will guarantee that your client isn't being served up things that are not the favored size. Utilizing Buying Intent Data to Turn Visitors into Customers The people who peruse.

BIGGYBOX Store Settings

Store settings allow you to set up the look of your online store and add products and functionalities as per your requirement.

Store Settings

Settings section allows you to configure different settings related to your store.

Settings are grouped into multiple subsections which are explained as below:

General Settings

General Settings allows you to configure general information about the store e.g. logo, store title, favicon, etc.

Addresses

Addresses allow you to add your store address and location.

Payment Settings

Payment settings allow you to configure the order related settings. e.g. minimum order value and order id prefix.

Payment Methods

Payment allows you to configure payment methods for your store. e.g. COD, Online Payment, etc.

Shipping

Shipping section allows you to manage shipping related settings.

User

User helps to configure settings related to users. You can setup user verification flow and other settings related to user registration.

Social Media

You can specify the links to your brand pages on different social media sites e.g. Facebook, Twitter, Linkedin, Instagram, Pinterest etc. The social media links can be shown on the Storefront for better user engagement.

Misc

It contains various miscellaneous fields for using in store for e.g. Webp Images

Seller Settings

Seller settings help to configure the admin panel for sellers

Shipping Methods

Shipping Methods allow you to set up shipping rates for the orders placed in your store.

Admin Users

Admin Users help you to create more logins to manage your store

Currencies

Multiple Currencies can be added through this feature e.g., INR, Dollar, etc

Translations

Translations helps to words for different languages e.g., Hindi, Myanmar, etc

Mail Notifications

Helps to create your own template for Mail notification for customers after an order is placed

Invoice Template

Helps to create your own invoice that would be generated to a customer

Conventional Msg (SMS) Notifications

You May Create Your Own Template For Conventional Msg Notification For Customers After An Order Is Placed. You Can Edit The Conventional Msg Notifications Only When You Are Using Own Custom Conventional Msg Gateway.

Domains

Manage your domains in this section. BiggyBox allows you to add multiple domains to your store.

SSL Certificates

You can manage SSL certificate in this section. BiggyBox offers free SSL certificates under most of its plans. You can also use your own SSL certificates.

Taxes

Depending on your product & Service, admin can add taxes that are applicable eg, sales, service etc

Languages

Configure the languages that you want your stores to be available in.

CONVENTIONAL MSG Provider

Multiple CONVENTIONAL MSG provider can be added to send notification to customers

Email Provider

Multiple Email provider can be added to send notification to customers

Delivery Pincodes

This is a feature where the admin can state which area the shipment can take place and on what payment method e.g. COD or Online payment or none.

Talk about the Unified Customer Experience at

Making a brought together client encounter crosswise over channels through a common archive of store and web based business information, and in addition striking an adjust on its web based business webpage amongst deals and marking, is a considerable measure of the concentration nowadays at attire retailer BiggyBox.

"What we need to do is available items to clients as reliably as conceivable from a cost and advancement point of view crosswise over channels," said Sellva, leader of internet business for BiggyBox, will's identity a keynote speaker on the subject at IRCE on June 9. "The entire idea of CRM is not new, but rather a considerable measure of retailers are attempting to catch data on clients and their exchanges at the purpose of offer, and have that information in an indistinguishable database from online buys, coordinating up client movement wherever they shop."

To enable it to arrive, Sellva said BiggyBox is not just consolidating cross-channel client into a solitary information ocean yet layering business knowledge on top to break down that information and better portion clients, accordingly interfacing with them in a more focused on, customized way. "For example in the event that we know somebody has purchased both from stores and on the web, they're probably going to be a superior client (regarding request esteem) than somebody who just purchased in one channel," Sellva said.

Including BI best of the of store and web based business exchange information from one area gives BiggyBox data like where a client is purchasing from (versatile, desktop, retail, and so forth.), at which stores, how as often as possible, what they're purchasing, and if it's essentially the maximum or marked down.

"There are generally extraordinary levels of data we can get to," he said. "As individuals tumble off the dynamic purchaser document, we need to elevate to them forcefully with reactivation informing, which is not the same as the individuals who are as yet purchasing in store. We need to have however much information as could reasonably be expected and mine it, all with the expectation of conveying more focused on informing than we may have the capacity to do today."

Sellva said the organization's online business website, replatformed two years back, is intended to strike a harmony amongst deals and marking. "Our old site was exceptionally trade situated in nature," he said. "Despite everything we need to offer, yet in addition need to expand the brand. We're not a major promoter, so we're utilizing our site to drive that."

Different activities at BiggyBox incorporate an adjustment of its storefront framework to include highlights and usefulness, particularly concerning catching information as noted above, and another versatile application that was propelled two months back.

BiggyBox's Using Technology to Transform the Customer Experience

Retailers need to concentrate less on the "gleaming new questions" in innovation and rather concentrate on frameworks and arrangements that really move the needle, said Sellva, founder for BiggyBox's, amid a component organize introduction at the webinar.

"Some of them are not attractive, but rather they enable us to work and change the business to be quicker and better," Sellva said. He said machine learning, counterfeit consciousness and chatbots – for both client and inside correspondence – are among the territories his advancement group is seeking after.

Sellva said BiggyBox's is trying chatbots for speaking with clients who have "where's my request" questions, and in addition secret word resets, a standout amongst the most well-known client benefit calls.

"Would we like to take four years on a task to change the store?" Sellva inquired. "No, however we are consistently changing the store understanding." for instance, he said BiggyBox's partners have an application with worked in knowledge that encourages them decide the ideal strategy for satisfying an online request in store.

As a separation from GoodDealSale, Sellva said the organization is propelling BiggyBox's Pay, a portable application that gives BiggyBox's cardholders a chance to join every one of their coupons, rebates and focuses with one sweep at checkout. BiggyBox's considers it to be an approach to expand the lifetime esteem and dependability of its clients by diminishing rubbing and expanding engagement.

"We are utilizing significantly more examination and machine figuring out how to make it an all the more convincing knowledge," Sellva stated, including Biggy Pay is being steered at multiple International. stores. "GoodDealSale is worked in an unexpected way. We chose to take care of an issue that is profoundly significant to our clients from an installment point of view, and it's the quickest approach to look at in our condition."

The organization still "has a profound association with Apple and Samsung" and will keep on collaborating on their versatile installment stages, despite the fact that those accomplices can't decide things like rebates and advancements at the SKU level, Sellva said.

"We're attempting to influence the store to encounter consistent, easy and drawing in," Sellva said. "The input on (Biggy Pay) has been phenomenal, and no other retailer is doing this."

BiggyBox's is likewise taking a shot at versatile innovation that will help clients all the more effectively explore the store and discover a thing speedier; that capacity is two or three years out, Sellva said.

On the web based business side, a current stage relaunch at BiggyBox's empowers things like machine learning and example acknowledgment to serve up query items in view of what item pages somebody went to. He said his group needs to convey KPIs like increments in change rate to legitimize the speculation. "Anything that doesn't function admirably, I challenge the group to improve the situation," Sellva said.

Portable Is One of the Top Initiatives for Retailers in current/not so distant future

In the midst of a seismic move in how International. buyers shop, retailers are competing for time on their clients' screens over every one of their gadgets — some time recently, amid and after a buy. That is as indicated by The State of Retailing Online current/not so distant future: Key Metrics, Business Objectives and Mobile report, discharged today by the National Retail Federation's Shop.org division and Forrester.

Forrester determined that in current year coordinate online deals totaled 11.6% of aggregate International. retail deals ($394 billion), however computerized touchpoints really affected an expected 49% of aggregate International. retail deals.

Accordingly, this year retailers are concentrating on a few key zones to improve client encounters over all touchpoints, developing their business as long as possible. For instance, x% of retailers take note of that versatile is one of their main three activities in current/not so distant future, as are showcasing (y%), site marketing (z%) and omni-stream endeavors (a%).

Among retailers reviewed, cell phones, by and large, made up 30% of online deals and 47% of online activity, and deals made on cell phones were up a normal of 65% year-over-year.

The investigation found that most retailers are previous conspicuous developing innovation, for example, virtual and expanded reality, and rather are putting resources into client encounter. Forty-five percent of retailers studied said portable activities changed their general computerized client experience, and client benefit beat the rundown of new activities retailers will put resources into throughout the following year, with highlights like live talk offering them a chance to associate with their clients.

"To develop, retailers know they need to work with a client fixated outlook to convey the encounters that buyers now expect at each touchpoint. It's tied in with having all parts of the business — stores, portable, promoting, client administration, satisfaction and that's only the tip of the iceberg — cooperate to convey add up to an incentive to your clients wherever they are, whenever."

Versatile Brings real markdown YoY Sales Growth for good begs

Good bags, a travel equip e-posterior and master reports that year over year deals through portable grew 70% for both Q4 and entire year current year while versatile movement grew 67% for Q4 and 53% for the year. Good Bags adjusted various activities around a Mobile First organization system which drove the positive outcomes.

"We're elated to report these numbers and salute the diligent work of our whole staff to guarantee clients reliably experienced enjoyment on the versatile channel," says Good Bags'. "Checkout rubbing is a noteworthy hindrance in versatile trade and we executed various activities to address this, we're glad to state, with extraordinary achievement."

> Reduced versatile checkout pages from 7 to 1

> Added versatile wallets (Apple Pay, ChasePay, MasterPass, Amex)

> Increased versatile site stack speed (a noteworthy obstacle for portable transformation)

> Incorporated versatile plan for site streamlining

> Fine-tuned messages to be less demanding for versatile clients

Likewise, the new Good Bags versatile application gives explorers access to novel instruments to enhance the voyage and keep them associated. The Good Bags Connected Luggage Tag is one development in the application that enables clients to keep their own data safe and rejoin with lost sacks. The Connected Tags are accessible in an assortment of styles and can be appended to a gear or sack.

Sellva as visionary made a remarks, "Good Begs' responsibility regarding offering an extensive portable answer for clients has been a key differentiator for us in the market today. We considered the particular needs and wants of our client base, which incorporated a quick affair, an assortment of installment choices, and a consistent way to buy from any gadget." He includes, "Furthermore, we realize that bob rates hop and transformation tumbles off forcefully for each extra second a site takes to stack. So versatile site speed is basic to an awesome client encounter. We have worked intimately with organizations like Yahoo and Google to survey and upgrade our versatile execution. Actually, a current Google appraisal checked that the Good Begs portable experience is best in class." As an example for product or online store front creator

Amid the festival season, my most loved channel to shop would be: I would need to state that I adore the sentiment festival soul and the main genuine approach to feel that will be out on the town at customary retail locations. Try not to misunderstand me, I cherish the funds of web based shopping, yet you truly can't beat the sounds and sights of the festival season.

Which matters more to you as a customer: Free Shipping, Same-day Shipping, Same-day Delivery and why: As a "need it now" buyer, I truly acknowledge same-day transportation and same-day conveyance. I am likewise ready to pay for it, since it spares me the bother of going out to the store to buy the thing I am searching for. In the event that I could take a shot at my understanding, free dispatching would be my first decision. Free dispatching truly influences the cost to hole amongst retail and online considerably more prominent and discernible.

When I'm not shopping individually site, my most loved place to shop is: About a year prior, I found the best fitting garments I have ever bought – shoes. Since that day, I infrequently timid far from shoes when I shop on the web.

Which computerized installment arrangement is acing the satisfaction procedure at the present time: There are a few advanced installment arrangements that are doing some extremely cool things at this moment, and in general, I would state that the customization bit of online business has been one of the coolest movements that I have seen. A standout amongst other wedding presents my significant other and I got a year ago was the highest point of a wine barrel that had our last name scratched into the wood and it originated from jualsell.com.

The greatest operations and satisfaction innovation upgrade I requirement for my business would be: At JualSell.com our deals have about multiplied every month since we propelled in November 2013 and our stock determining has been a noteworthy test. As a startup, income is the name of the amusement and it is hard to bolt a ton of capital into share. In this manner, we stroll as close of a line to without a moment to spare as we can, while maintaining a strategic distance from stock outs. There are a couple of programming arrangements in the market, however few appear to be precisely what we are searching for.

In my downtime, my most loved place to travel would be: My significant other and I cherish flying out to the wine nation in South Australia. Nothing beats a long end of the week loaded with the best sustenance and wine in the Australia!

The best exhortation I got from a manager, companion, tutor or relative is: As I was growing up, my dad ingrained the well known cheap cheap cheap cite in my vocabulary, "You will get all you need in life, on the off chance that you sufficiently enable other individuals to get what they need." This attitude is so valid and will drastically change your viewpoint and results on the off chance that you tail it, particularly in the event that you point it towards your clients. Overnight you will see connections bloom and deals rise.

When I'm was working, I have lived in Sydney, Australia for a little more than two years now and there are still such a large number of spots that I presently can't seem to visit in NSW. Each end of the week I attempt and investigate another region and see a greater amount of the excellence that Sydney brings to the table.

Achieve Facebook Users with New Autoplay Video

In case you're a devoted Facebook client you've presumably seen another element – when individuals post recordings that show up in your News Feed they start playing alone without you notwithstanding tapping on anything. This is a major headway in the Facebook and online video world: The interpersonal organization as of late declared that recordings that are transferred specifically to Facebook, or are shared from Instagram, are running in autoplay mode.

The autoplay work works a similar path on the Facebook versatile application – recordings begin playing naturally, but quieted until the point that you really tap on them, as you look down the page. When you pass the video it stops. After clients watch an autoplay video, they can observe more recordings from the same computerized installment arrangement.

I surmise that the autoplay highlight is an aid to advertisers who are endeavoring to pull in more eyeballs and produce all the more sharing on Facebook. It's a moderately calm method for conveying video about items or brands without making clients be irritated by a "meddling" video flying up out of the blue (and uproariously) on a website page they're perusing.

Facebook influenced an insightful move by quieting the recordings until clients to choose to tap on them. Online clients as a rule aren't content with recordings that begin playing – with sound – when they haven't picked in to review. It's an interruption on their perusing background and it doesn't influence them to think benevolently about the brands that are pushing the video. From my point of view, in light of the fact that autoplay recordings don't meddle with the Facebook encounter clients will probably react to marked recordings all the more decidedly.

Online advertisers may need to change the way they introduce recordings, being that Facebook has changed the standards. For instance, recordings without sound will require more alluring visuals to propel clients to tap on them and get the full involvement. A decent tip is to watch your recordings with the sound off, the way a Facebook client would see them. Would they be justified regardless of a tick or is it hard to make sense of what the video is about with no stable? In the event that your recordings don't recount a story outwardly, at that point they'll should be improved for the "noiseless" Facebook condition.

One approach to incorporate visual enthusiasm with your recordings is to include content, which can bolster the visuals. For instance, include a standard or looking over content that features an advancement, for example, a markdown. Consider saying that the arrangement is a Facebook select, as an additional motivating force to snap and watch.

Facebook's autoplay recordings may turn into an exceptionally significant piece of your web based promoting endeavors, particularly for more youthful clients: Facebook says that it can contact a larger number of individuals 18 to 24 years of age than Specialtime TV can – also those 870 million clients who take a gander at their news bolsters. For both expanding viewership of video and boosting social sharing, Facebook autoplay video is a decent component to have in your showcasing toolbox.

Utilizing Big Data to Improve Contact Center Operations

While huge information may appear like it by and large falls into the storehouse of the promoting division, more advanced installment arrangements are discovering that in addition to the fact that it is similarly as advantageous in the contact focus, yet it could likewise give you an edge against your rivals.

Contact focus experts, as per this infographic from ICMI, are discovering that huge information, otherwise called noteworthy information, can reach focus more proficient and lift client engagement. Truth be told, 69% of contact focus experts revealed to IMCI that they utilize this noteworthy information to enhance their contact focus operations by and large and 85% said that by giving their specialists access to client contact information has lessened excess CRM records.

Sellers

Register, add, edit or manage sellers on your multi-seller marketplace.

Sellers

der Sellers section, you can manage sellers who sell products on your store. Every stores has at least one seller. When you create a store on BiggyBox, a default seller is automatically created who is same as the store administrator.

To access Sellers section, go to Settings -> Sellers in BiggyBox Admin Panel.

Multi Seller Stores

BiggyBox allows merchants to convert their store into multi seller marketplaces. That means merchant can invite other sellers to sell their products on their stores. BiggyBox provides comprehensive tools for Admin to manage sellers and for sellers to manage their orders.

Multi Seller functionality is available only in Business and Enterprise Plans.

Little shops or Dealers to wind up internet business get and drop-off focuses

Online business organizations have thought of an intriguing answer for handle the difficulties of last-mile conveyance. One of the greatest difficulties that dispatch representatives confront while going out to convey merchandise, is that if a client is not promptly accessible to acknowledge the item, they need to persistently visit the client's home till the item can get conveyed. Following a couple of days however, the request consequently gets scratched off and the item gets came back to the merchant. Since there is no physical point where these items can be grabbed by the client if an item conveyance is missed, it ends up noticeably hard to arrange.

Online retailers are currently wanting to rope in little neighborhood shops and corner stores to help with last mile conveyance. As indicated by hypotheses, these will soon progress toward becoming get and drop-off focuses for online item conveyances.

India Post is additionally offering its areas as a component of this web based business design. It had effectively tied up with GoodDealSale and BiggyBox a half year prior. Regardless of around 90% of the division's more than unique post workplaces being in the provincial regions, pioneer (innovation) clarifies where independent logistics needs, "However major player like DHL/FEDEX/EMS?etc.. in unmatchable as far as exactness and entrance, online business relies upon snappy turnaround and conclusion of exchanges. This is the place outsider coordination's players remain to pick up."

Plan Executed

Major player Courier and Cargo intend to expand their range through this strategy, by appointing little corner shops close to the clients as get focuses for the items. "The issue of shut entryways in urban zones and also achieving level 3 and 4 urban areas for conveyance can be explained through get and drop-off focuses. Despite the fact that our inclination is for channel accomplices, we are chipping away at tie-ups with comfort stores, medicinal shops where our system is not accessible."

This idea is just been put without hesitation by "Just Ping" brand, the recent coordination's arm of online retailer BiggyBox. This venture is as of now being gone for crosswise over multiple countries. Sellva the author of this book and founder says, "The most imperative factor is to educate the client with reference to how the item will be conveyed. stores front will be paid a set expense, subtle elements of which are up in the air."

This is genuinely an inventive answer for the last mile conveyance challenge!

Worldwide Business to Business Process between Purchasing Goods from Cross-Border Ecommerce Marketplaces

Perform Periodical Evaluation and Reviews about Past Sales and Dealer Information

Checking surveys and remarks from past purchasers, and the measure of exchanges that a merchant has led on the stage can give a solid thought of the merchant's validity and execution. For instance, any web based business webpage, purchasers particularly rate merchant s in four classifications: things as depicted, correspondence, conveyance time, and sending charges. We generally prescribe that purchasers select merchant s with positive surveys.

Check the Rank of the Dealer

For instance, Ecommerce site positions merchants who lead business on their stage and place them into three classifications, in slipping request they are: top rank, medium rank, and normal rank. In the event that a merchant does not have a rank, at that point they have not yet met all requirements to wind up plainly a Top, fantastic, or normal rank. Top or more medium rank merchant have built up themselves as trustworthy by understanding a lot of exchanges and have gotten positive audits from the vast majority of those exchanges, and are in this way more prone to give higher quality items and administration.

If it's not too much trouble understand that the quantity of remarked by purchaser exchanges directed by a merchant makes the merchant's appraising more solid. The more exchanges a merchant has, the more that are figured into their rank, thusly a merchant with a positive rank who has led a ton of exchanges is more noteworthy than a merchant with a best rank with great surveys.

Internet business website really gives an item recording highlight that causes indexed lists to show up in dropping request in view of the merchant's rank. Simply check the "customer opinion" tick while hunting down things or merchandise comes about.

Comments the Merchandise or Goods Description Section

Internet business webpage prescribes that all Consumers to survey the "item antiques" range to affirm products subtle elements. This area incorporates: "item specifics," which will give the status, amount per deal, measurement, and other data particular to the products; "Returns and discount ensure points of interest" which detail the guidelines particular to the merchant ; and finally "antiques," which gives the merchandise depiction, the thing serial no, the genuine things name, the weight and different specifics.

Consumer Opinion the Logistics Services

To hoist idealize mindfulness, Ecommerce site prescribes that buyers dependably affirm the cost to convey the item and the time it will take for the merchandise to convey. For instance, on Ecommerce site, the "conveyance $" territory will give the assessed lead time and diverse expenses depending request sizes. The "conveyance lead Time and Cost" territory enables you to choose the correct conveyance administrations you need (worldwide suppliers), their costs, and assessed calculated lead time.

Understand How Common Consumer Issues Are Resolved On the Platform

Internet business website prescribes that all client completely comprehend the client benefit systems, and how contradictions are settled on the cross-fringe or worldwide web based business stage they are utilizing. On Ecommerce site, that data can be found from the accompanying connections: after deals benefit level targets, consistence and contract.

How to Contact the Dealer

On the off chance that purchasers need more itemized data about an item, or on the off chance that they need a positive assurance about an item's material, measurement, or produce process, Ecommerce website recommends that they contact the merchant straightforwardly through a correspondence medium or online visit. On the off chance that you are utilizing Ecommerce site, a record of all discussions is kept by the contradictions to after deals bolster group.

Quadrant of Ecommerce Player will Successfully in Providing Customer Experience

Endeavor client desires have been raised. It's about a client encounter where everything that goes into the way toward purchasing an item or administration matters. Regardless of whether that client returns or alludes you to others relies upon their client encounter.

Sponsorship that is an giant consulting firm ponder where 79% of B2B officials were persuaded the client experience or post deals s they give directly affects business comes about while 78% trusted it gives an upper hand.

It's extraordinary to have faith in, yet it's something else to really accomplish a vital client encounter. A similar report expressed just 23% of these B2B organizations thought they were making a viable showing with regards to. A B2B International investigation found even less administrators (14%) who trusted they were winning at their client encounter endeavors.

Thus lies the situation: How can B2B advertisers be effective at the client encounter?

Here are four ways that B2B advertisers can hold their clients returning for additional:

View the client encounter from back to front

Most organizations believe it's just about front aligned faculty and procedures, however the back end has an immense part to play. Consider it a theater execution. On the off chance that you place everything into the performers yet nothing into the view, ensembles, lighting and music, there's very little for the crowd to draw in with and no genuine experience. Hence, you have to survey what you can be doing in the background to upgrade the impact you convey through your site and other advertising channels (engineers, fashioners, and substance authors), your visit to their organization (deals staff, technologists, and advertisers), or you're showcasing guarantee (handouts, lists and evaluating sheets.)

Use new promoting innovation to develop advertising computerization and personalization

Despite the fact that the B2B client encounter is more about building connections, regardless you have to hope to advertising innovation that computerizes a significant part of the procedure for you. This gives you more opportunity to chip away at the human dynamic and engagement process with each organization. The key is to discover the innovation arrangement that is most appropriate to empower client encounter activities and can convey the focusing on and division required for progress.

Keep up disconnected channels

Conventional showcasing capacities still issue on the grounds that only one out of every odd buyer and business is exclusively shopping in the computerized world. Regardless of the possibility that they do shop on the web, there will be circumstances where you will likewise meet them face to face or where they will go over your image in their day by day lives. Here is the place preparing and an attention on social engagement procedures can have a critical effect in how a client sees their involvement with you.

Concentrate on tending to business torment focuses

Envision how your business clients will feel when they find you know precisely what damages and how you can reduce that torment for them. In the event that you can make your promoting messages and catch up with conveying on those guarantees, you make a significant ordeal where they consider you to be putting forth care, comfort, and the essential remedy for what upsets them. The following agony point that goes along, you can rely on them making a meeting with you.

It's tied in with Riding the Special Day Wave for Practical

At the point when the principal Special Day went along last July, healthy skin item organization Practical was genuinely new to B2B2C leaders, having quite recently joined the commercial center the past February. Around then, the emphasis was on raising the online profile of the 25 to 30 line expansions outside its center skin inflammation counteractive action item, which was esteemed a win.

For current year, the organization intends to advance its top rated items and ride the gigantic tidal wave of consideration and shopping movement the artificial shopping occasion has made.

Test said as a brand concentrated on coordinate showcasing through infomercials, mailings and email, Practical must be mindful so as not to tear up deals that channel through Special Day and its B2B2C leaders nearness. "So it was an instance of stroll before I run," he said.

Saying Practical is "not the sort of product offering individuals are clamoring to discover when there's a major deal," Sample said Special Day past year was regardless a win. "The expanded movement allowed us to get before many people who didn't know they ready to purchase our item on B2B2C leaders," he said. "That was the enormous takeaway a year ago."

"So we're watchful about what we advance and not contending with ourselves," Sample said. "Since we have some involvement on the stage, we have a superior feeling of who's purchasing what items, and what affect it has on whatever remains of the business. Presently we feel more certain that we're managing distinctive clients on B2B2C leaders, and can deal with the channel more autonomously than we did some time recently."

Portable, Personalization, Relevance Key to Revolutionary at BiggyBox

Retailers need to a greater extent a portable first mindset, a high level of personalization and a solid dedication center on the off chance that they will reach, draw in and hold Generation Y customers, as indicated by Sellva, leader of online business for youth clothing firm BiggyBox.

Sellva's view "We're not there today, but rather we have to arrive. Maybe it includes reengineering from an innovation viewpoint, utilizing a similar code base for desktop and versatile. Search for approaches to change your innovation for portable, making it snappier and less demanding to shop."

Sellva viewed BiggyBox propelled a portable application in the previous month, and has seen versatile movement increment in the vicinity of 15% and 30%, however changes aren't there yet. "At the point when a client is on portable, they're not perusing item as much as on desktop, and the normal request is a bit lower," he said. "We have to strive to make sense of how they can peruse rapidly and effectively (on versatile) and increment the request measure."

Unwaveringness is likewise an immense need at Steven Madden, Sellva stated, during a time when purchasers bounce considerably simpler and speedier from brand to mark. With that in mind, the organization will soon reveal a dependability program in which clients gain focuses for cool advantages like giving their contribution at a BiggyBox configuration focus or meeting BiggyBox himself.

"Product of Beauty, for instance, has had solid income of late, and they gab about dedication – what number of individuals, what number of drew in, what number of dynamic," he said. "Faithful clients are the best and generally productive. They need to feel a piece of your image. It's stunning what they send us on Instagram. They take shots make a beeline for toe in a styled outfit, and take pride in being a piece of BiggyBox."

Sellva included that unwaveringness is not just about the amount they spend, "it's the way you treat them once they say yes."

The more customized the experience, the more the client is locked in with the brand and discovers significance. "Nothing is more vital (than personalization) if concentrating on Generation Y clients, however truly with everybody," he said.

With its fun vibe and youth center, online networking is obviously a major piece of BiggyBox's promoting approach, however there's space to develop, Sellva said. The organization has over 1 million supporters on Instagram and 1 million on Facebook. "Each touchpoint needs to associate, however honestly there's a considerable measure of space to enhance, regardless of actuality that our client base is exceptionally social sagacious," he said. "Client created content appears to work ridiculously well. The greater engagement with consumer, the higher the spend."

Regarding innovation coordination, Sellva said many organizations are as yet attempting to incorporate heritage frameworks to more up to date ones to meet omnichannel requests. "We replatformed in coming years, and it resembled appending PVC pipe to elastic pipe without any strings," he said.

"Omni-Stream technique is difficult to execute however it works. BiggyBox was doing ship from stores before I

He additionally said that BiggyBox has become past the point where it was worried about the cannibalization of store deals through web based business, seeing it rather as an advantageous two-way road. "The in-store encounter spares the deal by supporting customers who are going on the web," he said. "When we advertise online it drives individuals to stores, while great client involvement in the store drives them to online buys."

How Brands Can Build Trust with Generation Y?

Dissimilar to Gen Z, Generation Y are not computerized locals. They recollect a world before solid web, and when hanging out at the shopping center for entertainment only was the cool thing to do. Yet, as advances enhanced and the web played a focal part in trade, Generation Y immediately received computerized as a way to better educate their buy choices in light of value, quality, and social obligation.

They are an unequivocal gathering, positive about their preferences, and unafraid to impart their insights with companions via web-based networking media. For retail advertisers to be fruitful in contacting them, brands must present their incentive in a real way that meets Generation Y desires.

Certain, Spendthrift Purchasers

In spite of transitioning amid the Great Recession and being confronted with understudy obligation, 60% of Generation Y distinguish as "spenders" or "enormous spenders." This isn't to state they toss their cash around, the same number of likewise recognize as wise customers who value contrast and screen their most loved retailers with only shop deals. They're willing to spend more cash on important buys or on brands that show an incentive through endeavors like inventive plan or natural awareness.

As a result of these inclinations, numerous retailers are attempting to remain pertinent as more youthful customers advance toward brands that are more reasonable. J.Crew swung to forceful markdowns and "super deals" to pull in more value delicate customers after the brand was esteemed overrated, and unintentionally prepared its clients to hold up until the point that items went on advancement to make a buy. This strategy neglected to change client view of the brand's esteem, and reaffirmed that its items are never worth buying at the maximum.

Be that as it may, for brands like Apple, whose personality has turned out to be synonymous with helpful inventiveness and uniqueness on the back of its smooth outline and capable working frameworks, Generation Y won't dither to buy new stock at the maximum. For whatever length of time that Apple's image is seen with that same uplifting store, it will keep on finding accomplishment inside the associate.

Generation Y do their examination to discover items that meet their certain requirements at the correct cost. Brands that unmistakably exhibit their esteem, either through sensible value focuses or by making an incentive through a one of a kind brand personality, will associate unequivocally with the statistic. For advertisers, this implies unmistakably exhibiting what a brand conveys to the table in a way that is relatable, engaging, and encourages reliability.

The Friend Factor

Brands that show esteem and have a relatable brand story should next reach Generation Y in a way that feels true. 80% of Generation Y detailed they acknowledge advertisements when they're set well, and will even share a promotion they find entertaining with their informal communities. Viral advertising resounds with Generation Y as honest; companions helping companions by sharing an item they like or a message they find interesting or persuasive.

Achieving Generation Y where they share news and exhortation with companions via web-based networking media channels like Facebook, Instagram, and Snapchat brings your image into the setting of their social lives, and makes a discourse with your client. For those brands that carry identity alongside a one of a kind story to the table, anything is possible. Generation Y will share items that reverberate with their companions, enabling viral promoting to wind up plainly a honest to goodness part of your advertising design.

That sentiment relatability and genuineness must resound past your image's web-based social networking channels, notwithstanding. With the end goal for Generation Y to genuinely confide in your image, the message must be clear and reliable crosswise over wherever your item shows up – this implies in store, in publicizing, and on portable. Without this consistency, Generation Y will see your image as pandering and inauthentic.

Feel Good Purchases

Generation Y are additionally intrigued by social obligation, and value knowing items are outlined, created, and sent with the welfare of workers and more noteworthy's benefit at the top of the priority list. Brands that have influenced a one of a kind sense of duty regarding a particular social reason, to like being earth benevolent or offering back to the group, encourage goodwill with Generation Y who are glad to vote with their dollars.

Maybe most eminently, footwear mark TOMS shoes began a basic "one for one" guarantee, giving one sets of shoes or eyewear for each thing acquired. The brand's prevalence enabled it to develop its business and charitable endeavors to help disappointed groups around the world. By making data about socially honest activities accessible in-store or on the web, brands can guarantee Generation Y know about their social situating, bringing them into the overlap of the mission of the organization, and giving them a vibe decent story they can tell their companions.

Making a Unified Brand Experience

Brands that set aside the opportunity to be straightforward about the esteem and advantage of their items, while additionally genuinely attempting to improve the world a place, will make an affair that wins the profound respect, and spending, of Generation Y. Advertisers must make sure to set up a steady, directed brand story that imparts esteem, validness, and kindness to see genuine progress with this statistic.

What Retailers Need to Know About Generation Y' Mobile Shopping Habits?

For retailers to comprehend a decent amount of the present market, they should comprehend the versatile shopping propensities one of the greatest eras today – Generation Y.

Twenty-eight percent of Generation Y like to shop internet utilizing cell phones than a desktop PC. This infographic by Coupofy features why and how Generation Y are utilizing their cell phone gadgets.

Inquiry Data Reveals What Generation Y Moms Want for Mother's Day

Mother's Day is quickly drawing nearer and regardless of the way that there's been an unfaltering ascent in Mother's Day-related quests since mid-April, around 70 percent of Mother's Day-centered online movement will happen amid the most recent week before the huge day, as indicated by an examination by Hitwise, a division of Connexity.

While Gen X ladies still record for the biggest offer of mothers bringing up kids, Generation Y mothers are quickly expanding their positions and you can wager that this era of dynamic, well informed mothers will be expecting more than blossoms and breakfast in bed.

Blessing thoughts to enable Generation Y mothers to remain fit: Buying a mother of all ages a standard rec center enrollment might be deciphered in the wrong way and land the blessing provider in heated water. These wellness related thoughts obliged Generation Y mothers' interests are a significantly more secure wager.

> ClassPass: Available in a developing number of urban communities, ClassPass, or a comparative sort of pass that enables the client to take classes at different range exercise centers might be straight up mother's rear way. Truth be told, Generation Y mothers are five times more probable than the normal lady to look for "ClassPass" on the web.

Vinyasa Yoga: Generation Y are once in a while content with the standard anything; they need something extraordinary. Consider purchasing a couple of classes from a Vinyasa yoga studio since Generation Y mothers are three times more inclined to scan for data on this particular style of yoga than the normal lady.

Blessing thoughts to enable Generation Y mothers to loosen up or connect to: Generation Y mothers are the most associated ever so risks are, she as of now has every one of the gadgets she needs. Be that as it may, why not help her benefit as much as possible from them… or enable her to isolate when she needs a break.

Spotify Premium or Pandora One: Generation Y became an adult in the period of Internet radio, so why not give Generation Y mothers the endowment of boundless, advertisement free music spilling to keep her sticking day and night—regardless of the possibility that it is to that baby music station. On the off chance that you don't, she'll need to get it herself. Generation Y mothers are 79 percent more inclined to look for Spotify Premium and twice as prone to scan for Pandora One.

B2B2C pioneers Echo, Dot or Tap: More than only a remote speaker, the recently extended B2B2C pioneers Echo line of items enables associated mothers to complete stuff without hands. Generation Y mothers are as of now 50 percent more probable than normal to scan for the first B2B2C pioneers Echo and are much more prone to be examination shopping between the new Dot and Tap.

Essential oils: Even technically knowledgeable mothers require time to unplug. What's more, numerous Generation Y mothers are searching out the calming and recuperating forces of basic oils. Scans for "basic oil" are five times more noteworthy among Generation Y mothers than among ladies when all is said in done, and driving oil maker to gets a 52 percent more noteworthy offer of online visits from Generation Y mothers than normal.

Blessing thoughts to loan Generation Y mothers a hand: What on the off chance that you could give mother the endowment of time? A developing number of organizations offer membership boxes that guarantee to both spare the beneficiary time yet in addition astonishment and joy. Giving a Generation Y mother a membership to one of the organizations beneath should give her back a couple of minutes in her day and put a grin all over.

Steps to a More Effective, Holistic Omnichannel Strategy

Retailers normally center their omnichannel abilities with laser-like accuracy on client confronting capacities.

It's a decent begin. In any case, many battle to keep up solid edges since they neglect to match up with the key offices and procedures that clients never straightforwardly connect with. Marketing, coordinations, showcasing and arranging divisions all assume a key part in the collection, evaluating and advancements that impact customer encounter. Without their support, endeavors to make consistent client encounters can crash and burn — thus can benefits.

Call it chronicled oversight. A while ago when omnichannel was only a glimmer in retailers' eyes, starting internet business endeavors regularly ran parallel to – and free of – customary physical help operations. Rather than one all-encompassing vision, there were two. The online specialty unit and physical specialty unit frequently wound up with no solidified money related arranging and no methodology for sharing stock. Omnichannel expects retailers to close those holes.

Here are 6 stages for molding a more all-encompassing way to deal with omnichannel methodology that can help advance edges by effectively including promoting, coordinations and arranging:

Set up cross-utilitarian groups

For an effective omnichannel operation, the hierarchical boundaries need to descend over all advanced and physical channels. Officials need to help promoting with working gatherings that unite individuals from advertising, production network, coordinations and stock arranging groups.

Redesign promoting with clear parts/obligations

Hierarchical structure and credit for deals can be a problem area for interior fights. To guarantee corporate concentrate on shared objectives, build up an adaptable structure that incorporates regular groups for purchasing, arranging, and purchaser bits of knowledge, and additionally to price, advancements, and markdowns. Note that retailers are additionally rebuilding to adjust their promoting and showcasing capacities. For instance, social domain has consolidated its on the web and store promoting and arranging groups.

Another region of center is around making omnichannel possession and guaranteeing official help for channel arrangement and union. The Finish Line COCO reports straightforwardly to the President and is in charge of all client confronting touchpoints including computerized, store operations, the client mind focus and brand advertising.

Put resources into IT and business forms

Fortunately retailers are improving at dealing with the IT and business-process suggestions for upgrading the client encounter. Be that as it may, there stay numerous chances to bring more prominent efficiencies. For instance, the well known administration of enabling clients to purchase items on the web and lift them up in stores is trying for retailers' request arranging and satisfaction operations. A far reaching audit of client inclinations with fitting business and IT improvements to address their issues can help smooth the procedure for retailers and customers alike.

Build up an objective arranged motivation structure

Departmental objectives frequently divert from the mission of omnichannel associations. Retailers' predominant channels, regardless of whether in-store or on the web, frequently elbow out their littler partners and can prompt infighting. Fortify the omnichannel approach by binds rewards to general corporate numbers instead of particular specialty unit objectives.

Embrace persistent, ongoing arranging

Retailers can never again design inside storehouses bound by manufactured "occasional" time periods. Rather, arranging societies must separate the storehouses and embrace nonstop, constant procedures that foresee and conform to showcase changes as they happen — whether mid-season, post-season, early season or late. By actualizing a cross-channel, incorporated arranging process, retailers can mix dexterity and knowledge into the venture and enhance responsiveness, expect slants and grow edges.

Keep in mind to get ready for the social changes

Adjusting retail culture to help omnichannel operations is particularly testing. Change administration is significant. To make official champions for channel arrangement and union, retailers, for example, BiggyBox luxury items and The Finish Line have added boss omnichannel officers to the C-suite.

Omnichannel implies one organization, one group. By changing their focal point to center far reaching and in addition on client touchpoints, retailers can make the channel-freethinker stock arranging process that is fundamental to omnichannel achievement.

Omnichannel Crystal Ball

What will retail look like in 2014? While customer robots won't show up in each store one year from now, we're obviously made a beeline for another period in retail robotization, one that is certain to totally change the client encounter.

Similarly as Ford reformed assembling via robotizing the mechanical production system, mechanization advancements – combined with the quickening combination of the disconnected and online universes – will overturn the retail business start to finish.

In 2014, I see two major patterns developing: the ascent of the universal customer and wide-scale retail robotization.

The Ubiquitous Shopper

The pervasive customer is an idea that ties together area based versatile information, back-end client frameworks, for example, buy and CRM databases, and clients' advanced and social impression to make a one of a kind "picture" of every customer. This versatile client profile makes a more individual shopping background for every client – enabling purchasers to be "perceived" while in-store much like an advanced mother and-pop store involvement. Similarly treats and other following innovation guarantee you're once in a while unknown on the web, Wi-Fi, GPS and other rising advances will do a similar thing in-store.

It may look something like this. A client strolls into a store, is promptly perceived, and accordingly gets cautions for customized advancements in light of his past buy history and social/computerized movement. As the customer strolls around the store, Wi-Fi following and geo-fencing keep on customizing the shopping background. At the point when the client looks at, the clerk gets a look at his buy history and his profile – making a feeling of individualized client benefit. At the point when a similar client sign onto the retailer's webpage, customized offers and data will seem on the web.

What's to come is clear: one shopping knowledge over all channels

Obviously, the majority of this action would be 100% select in. I trust an ever increasing number of purchasers will pick into programs like this – in light of the fact that they result in a predominant shopping knowledge. Furthermore, every time a client communicates with a retailer in a store, on its site, or by means of online networking channels, that information will be added to the client's "profile" – making a more exact photo of a buyer after some time.

Effectively, some ground breaking omnichannel retailers are exploring different avenues regarding omnipresent customer profiles. For instance, Lowe's keeps client buy history unified, regardless of where you buy an item. Say a client is obtaining a substitution wire for a weed-whacker at a Lowe's store. At checkout, the representative can see a depiction of his buy history and may see he already purchased an alternate width of wire on the web. She could say he may have erroneously gotten the wrong size – sparing him the cerebral pain of returning home just to acknowledge he bought the wrong thing. Amazing.

Retail Automation

The ascent of the universal customer runs as one with the second enormous retail pattern of 2014: robotization. The greater part of US buyers now have cell phones, and they convey their cell phones with them consistently. So it bodes well retailers would start to take off in-store advances that use cell phones to robotize a ton of undertakings beforehand done by people, for example, prescribing items, giving more data on items, or assisting with store route.

For instance, it will end up noticeably typical for retailers to offer readable scanner tags, empowering customers to promptly get more data on items, rather than attempting to find a partner who could conceivably think about the item. Stores will offer area mindful portable applications that perceive which store a customer is in, in a split second introducing an accessible store format for simple route.

Different stores will take off in-store tablet requesting booths to enable clients to buy items for prompt pickup at an exceptional self-checkout work area. While a genuine individual may at present be important to find the thing in the stockroom, that procedure could soon be robotized with a robot and a transport line. Furthermore, there's no reason a store couldn't utilize GPS following to "perceive" a customer when he maneuvers into the store parking garage, and after that have his online request holding up at an exceptional checkout work area the minute he arrives. The customer may likewise get a moment coupon redeemable in-store for items he'd probably buy, in light of his compact client profile.

One note: store partners aren't leaving. There will dependably be a part for people in the shopping knowledge. However, staff will invest less energy in unremarkable errands like checkout, restocking, and giving essential item data, and additional time going about as 'mark ministers' to influence the store to encounter fun and locks in.

Maybe we're still years from robots hurrying around stores, or automatons conveying B2B2C pioneers bundles, however we'll see the early strides toward this robotized future in 2014. Together, the take off of computerization and customer profiles will make a colossal new range of information for retailers to gauge and examine. As customers move from home to store and back once more, and as they peruse and buy stock utilizing as a part of store computerization frameworks, every collaboration turns into a quantifiable information point that enables retailers to illustrate every customer.

In 2014, the qualification amongst on the web and disconnected shopping will obscure further. Customers will locate the online experience mirrors the store, and the other way around – making shopping a consistent ordeal regardless of where they peruse and purchase.

Usability

The Shopping Habits of the B2B Buyer

With regards to the purchasing inclinations of B2B customers, providers need to begin making a web based shopping background like those in the B2C world. Interpretation: B2B sites should be anything but difficult to utilize. In this infographic from the Acquity Group you will realize precisely what sorts of B2B customers are out there, what their shopping propensities are, and how 71% of corporate purchasers say they would build the measure of cash spent on a B2B site on the off chance that it was less demanding to utilize.

Swapping out your first online business stage and changing to another one can be terrifying and overwhelming. So where do you start?

"In the event that you need to develop, you need to have robotization," "The simplicity of refreshing information is essential."

When contemplating what highlights you are thinking about, you ought to consider whether you need the capacity to have a list of things to get and how much information there will be on your new internet business stage.

In the event that you do in-house outline on your site, it is a considerably less demanding procedure, yet there is a higher cost. Be that as it may, in the event that you do it because of house you have less control, he said. Anderson suggests doing your own examination.

"You have to consider how you will progress your connections to another site," he told participants.

Sellva's view prescribes looking for additional assistance when choosing to dispatch another internet business stage.

Three things advanced installment arrangements need to consider when choosing to replatform, as indicated in typical business arrangement, is minimum amount, the checking procedure, and progress and execution.

"Too huge is typically excessively costly," when pondering the checking procedure of replatforming, "be cool in keeping deals where they are."

On the off chance that you are pondering replatforming, you will need think about the cost and whether you will need to have SEO on the site.

While progressing, delineate arrangement before you sign on to replatform and have an alternate course of action, as indicated by Sellva.

Tips for Selecting Your Next Ecommerce Platform

Advanced installment arrangements that are hoping to supplant their current web based business stages may observe it to be a staggering errand. With such huge numbers of decisions accessible, how would you choose which online business stage best suits your web based business needs?

Get Yourself a Request for Proposal

The primary thing that advanced installment arrangements need to consider while choosing another web based business stage is the Request for Proposal. As you begin composing your RFP, consider what you will do to think about merchants and their reactions. The next to each other cost and usefulness examination is critical to the basic leadership process.

Create a List of Vendors

Build up a short rundown of sellers who will get your RFP. This rundown ought to be between three to five firms. The short rundown ought to be a result of research and a pre-capability process that you and your group have done ahead of time.

Include a Non Disclosure Agreement

The RFPs ought to incorporate Non-Disclosure Agreement, marked ahead of time, a contact individual inside your organization who is assigned to answer any inquiries concerning the RFP itself, and an end date in which they have to answer to the RFP by. These things sound rudimentary however they are basic in getting an auspicious RFP reaction.

Remember Site Expectations

Bear in mind to incorporate the things that you need to see on your new site in the RFP. This ought to incorporate focuses, for example, enhancing ease of use, refresh outline, and increment deals through better designs, and better substance control.

Illustrate Your Site Requirements

While it is vital to advise the merchant what you need to see on your site, it's likewise critical to indicate them. Represent what highlights and capacities that you see as a necessity on your new site and give the merchant particular cases of locales that you believe are doing it well. Consequently, request that the merchant give you particular customer cases for each of your prerequisites.

Always Include Marketing Expectations

Make sure to inquire as to whether they have experts on staff (or organizations together with advisors) that can help you in showcasing advancements, increment normal request measure, diminish truck deserting, and enhance SEO and natural inquiry. These inquiries should be asked in your RFP.

Have a Plan Ready

Merchants need to know going ahead what the RFP procedure for your organization will resemble. Be sure about the time allotment you expect on everything from marking the agreement to when the site will go live. This will end up being the reason for judging the seller's capacities, expenses, and capacity to convey.

Tips on SEO Tactics

Thoughts to be clarified amid the session that SEO is not about watchwords and rankings, its about understanding your objective market and situating your site to be there when they're hunting down you. What's more, its understanding the genuine ROI of different SEO strategies and methodologies.

The two speakers offered these Tips on Tried and True SEO Tactics:

Interior Education – Lean on your organization. Take into consideration SEO to wind up some portion of discussion. Teach your organization, over-impart ensuring everybody is on your group. You'll need to utilize visuals to drive motivation to the client.

Devote Resources – Lack of usage is the main source of SEO disappointment. From a brand point of view, don't expect execution without completing stuff and from an organization viewpoint, be a venture chief.

Make Advocates – From senior authority, from the improvement group; (outside SEO group is ideal) it helps positioning contentions.

Demonstrate ROI – You have information, measure it. Demonstrate some sort of results, take a gander at activity and deals. At last natural movement and income is the thing that you need to be following on a natural level, utilize innovation.

Google+ Matters – Invest in a Google+ mark page and change to make it one of a kind to your image. There are approaches to comprehend the estimation of Google+ long haul. Google+ incorporates with Google look. Google+ will demonstrate to you your identity and your identity associated with.

Cure (not gave) – There is a cure to the "not gave." 33% of Google seek questions are covered up. The cure is that "not gave" data is promptly accessible by utilizing Google Web Master devices. Audette suggests utilizing Google Analytics. Advanced installment arrangements need to know the "not gave" data is as yet accessible. Likewise, when utilizing Google Analytics, take a gander at it once every month.

Change Your Philosophy – Think about SEO recently. Concentrate on individuals not on web crawlers. There are a few misguided judgments about SEO:

> Misconception 1 – Focus on the calculations. Cure – concentrate on the client to start with, last and dependably. Concentrate on the esteem.

> Misconception 2 – Focus on the watchwords. Cure – Understand your market portion and comprehend your identity attempting to target and pulling it in through a web search tool.

> Misconception 3 – Focus on rankings. Cure – Know what measurements matter. Frequently rankings don't make a difference.

Content Strategy – Create an incredible ordeal online with great substance. Nourish the substance into your own particular data engineering.

Google Revamping Shopping Experience through Analytics

BiggyBox Service, as indicated by the discharge, utilizes investigative instruments that measures and rates "the conclusion to-end benefit understanding crosswise over help channels including telephone, email, talk and Twitter and delivering, returns and discounts" of retailers. Those measurements additionally incorporate speed of contact focus and bundling quality.

"We're centered around making it simple for individuals to discover precisely what they need at the best online stores," he said in the discharge.

Shipments

Shipment is a fundamental understanding of ecommerce or digital business and in my digital transformation vision for BiggyBox or biggybox provides different options to ship customer orders. You can manage the shipments for your orders in Shipments Section in BiggyBox Admin Panel.

Under Shipments section, there are further sub sections

Shipments

Once the pickup for a shipment is arranged, you can manage shipments from the shipments section.

Shipping Adjustments

Shipping adjustments are applicable only when you are using Shippo services.

In certain scenarios, the shipping charges visible to you at the time of shipment might differ from what logitics providers charge at the time of billing. In this section you can manage the adjustments made to your shipping charges at the time of billing.

COD Ledger

You can also check the COD payments received and can also raise a withdrawal request.

Steps to a Better Third-Party Logistics Relationship

In helping multichannel organizations settle on outsider coordinations and contact focus choice, we have discovered many have possessed the capacity to develop their organizations productively by outsourcing.

Outsourcing is not for everybody. Numerous customers feel they need add up to control of client benefit, and that they can convey a lower cost for each request by taking care of satisfaction inside.

However, for those that utilization a 3PL, here are 5 ways we have seen various customers get the most out of the outsourcing relationship, including for contact focus administrations. Some of these focuses need to wind up some portion of the arrangement procedure and setting of desires from the earliest starting point.

Creating a "Win/Win" For Both Parties

I was chatting with a vast 3PL as of late about a planned customer, who said their normal customer has been with them 11 years. They have many offices and a large number of square feet of distribution center space in the INTERNATIONAL. furthermore, seaward. Consider that for a moment – that says a great deal in regards to finding the correct accomplice in a period when quality, administration and minimal effort are vital to your business, gainfulness and ROI for your partners.

In fact, "organization" has moved toward becoming abused. In any case, would you say you are really searching for a long haul organization and a stage to develop your business on, or for a minimal effort for every exchange benefit? Here are a few musings about this:

> Many littler 3PLs can just go up against a specific number of customers and process a given number of requests. Comprehend their business drivers. For instance, in satisfaction don't move their DC toward a parking area for moderate moving item; this may prompt higher expenses. Convenient liquidation of overload will be best for your business by making lean inventories.

From your point of view, what are the close term and long haul administrations you have to develop your business? These incorporate changes in promoting and guaging frameworks and business insight applications. Are there new frameworks and administrations your 3PL accomplice will put resources into to give better administrations to your organization?

Making a genuine association and win/win situation is the true objective; what do the two gatherings suspect and want?

Measuring Performance

We regularly observe organizations neglecting to influence quality and execution principles to some portion of the agreement. For beyond any doubt they are talked about in the business procedure, however should be formalized as a major aspect of the understanding.

You'll certainly have day by day dialogs about how the 3PL is getting the function out. In any case, senior administration for the most part likely delegates the everyday oversight to an organization contact. It's regularly simple to put some distance between the 10,000 foot view execution against the principles. As a component of the transaction procedure indicate the benchmarks, how they're characterized and how they'll be checked. What will you get as far as a dashboard or abridged operations reports?

Some contact focus measurements incorporate call deserting rate, benefit levels and cost parts. In satisfaction they incorporate cargo cost want to real, blunder rates, benefit levels against the standard (e.g. times for getting to secure, arrange turnaround and percent of requests delivered same day, returns handling) and cost per arrange.

As a feature of the transaction procedure, set up a scorecard way to deal with inspecting execution month to month or quarterly. Have a month to month 30-minute phone survey with administration. Each group should audit the scorecard and keep each other refreshed.

Regular On-Site Visits

You can't generally get the aggregate picture from the information. We have discovered that numerous clients of 3PL administrations don't make nearby visits as often as sufficiently possible. Some littler clients get more consideration for their record by becoming more acquainted with individuals taking a shot at their record by and by.

On location visits may likewise make it less demanding to talk about real changes your organization needs to make to methodology and strategies.

Another perspective to consider is the manner by which to consistently stay up with the latest as your stock combination changes. In the contact focus this incorporates specialist preparing. For satisfaction this can incorporate any adjustments in pressing and sending for new classifications of items, and discovering approaches to shield things from harm without unnecessary dimensional weight charges.

Provide Short-Term Planning and Forecasting

A huge number require progressing gauges (receipts, orders, shipments, and so on.) a few months ahead of time inside settled upon resistances. For organizations that have not done this well it may be viewed as prohibitive, however it's the main way the 3PL can guarantee it has the correct number of individuals accessible to benefit your record. Better arranging will likewise help your business.

Involve them in Your Long-Range Planning

Include the outsourcing supplier in your long-extend arranging. This incorporates early contribution in talks about conceivable acquisitions; new brands; changes in volume; significant changes in advertising; changes in stock grouping that may influence dimensional weight; and changes in investigation that may prompt IT overhauls.

These five exercises will incredibly upgrade your involvement with a 3PL accomplice, empowering them to give quality administrations at your expected expenses.

Approaches to Alleviate Frustration after a Tough Customer Interaction

Stock:

The most effective method to Finally Tame the Ecommerce Fulfillment Beast

It's difficult to trust it yet indeed, Operations Summit is upon us!

One week from now the group at Multichannel Digital installment arrangement is anxious to join 800+ experts from over the range of direct-to-client and online business operations and satisfaction at the David L. Lawrence Convention Center in Pittsburgh, PA for our fifth yearly occasion.

We have a stuffed program teed up for you. From office visits at FedEx, Giant Eagle and SEKO Logistics to our new innovation track, the third yearly Excellence in Customer Experience Awards and our five preconference workshops, there's a touch of something for everybody, and the sky is the limit from there.

Some of the current year's features:

> Keynote speakers: new this year, we'll be got notification from noted web based business store network master Jim Tompkins on the seismic effect of computerized disturbance, and how to address it. At that point Afterburner Inc. organizer and CEO Jim "Murph" Murphy, a previous INTERNATIONAL. Aviation based armed forces military pilot teacher, will discuss how to accomplish immaculate execution in your association.

> Top brands: Hear certifiable cases of how operational difficulties are being met and managed from our 100+ speakers, including administrators from Dick's Sporting Goods, Macy's, Hudson's Bay Co., Nordstrom, REI, McKesson and Lane Bryant, among others.

> New workshop: Cross-Border Strategies and Tactics. A specialist board will go inside and out on points like

how to fabricate your cross-outskirt shipping procedure and the most ideal approaches to source and vet neighborhood satisfaction and conveyance accomplices.

Welcome Party: Always a feature at Ops Summit, the Welcome Party on Monday night is an awesome place to get together with kindred participants, speakers, patrons and exhibitors, get a decisive advantage over your systems administration and make new contacts.

New innovation track: directed by Doug Brochu, author and CEO of Bridge Solutions Group, this new track will take an abnormal state perspective of frameworks and reconciliations covering WMS, OMS, stock administration and inventory network administration. Accompany inquiries and leave equipped with bits of knowledge!

As usual, there will be a lot of chance at Operations Summit to interface with industry peers, get reacquainted with companions and make profitable new contacts.

3 Key Retail Supply Chain Trends to Watch in current/not so distant future

A B2B2C pioneers official said the organization now is simply utilizing its current interests in coordinations and transportation to deal with interior limit, including overhauling merchant s utilizing its Fulfilled by B2B2C pioneers (FBA) program where it handles outsider requests.

"That limit will be accessible to outsiders," Paul Misener, VP of worldwide development strategy and interchanges for B2B2C pioneers, said as of late at Home Delivery World. "In case you're a FBA merchant with stock in our satisfaction focuses that should be moved. All the coordinations framework will be moving outsider items and retail items."

Misener said the sad Christmas season in 2013, when an ideal tempest of issues prompted around 1 million late conveyances, numerous from B2B2C pioneers itself, as the driving force for the coordinations push. He added

B2B2C pioneers keeps on working intimately with every one of the three noteworthy transporters, particularly the INTERNATIONAL. Postal Service. "We've affirmed before Congress when the USPS was thinking about cutting Saturday conveyance," Misener said. "We let them know, don't do that, include Sunday. That foundation was sitting inactive, and it enables us to better serve our clients."

Misener wouldn't remark on whether B2B2C pioneers wanted to utilize its current speculations – including the buy of load planes, tractor trailers and a noteworthy interest in sea cargo sending from China – to offer coordinations as its very own administration outside volume or FBA clients. This model has demonstrated amazingly lucrative on account of B2B2C pioneers Web Services.

Numerous onlookers have conjectured that "coordinations as an administration" is the organization's definitive objective, given these moves.

Examination

Retail supply chains are longer and more tangled than any other time in recent memory – the intricacy of the informational indexes and the administration of far-flung providers combined with high client desires around administration and dependability are burdening conventional ways to deal with store network administration as far as possible.

Production network administration assumes a huge part not just in a retailer's cost structure and gainfulness yet additionally in the nature of the client encounter. Purchasers will never again endure conveyance issues or out-of stock – retailers that can't satisfy immaculate request conveyance and interminably in stock can't depend on faithfulness to keep clients in the overlay.

The issue with conventional retail inventory network administration is three-crease. To start with, existing arrangements can't convey end-to-end perceivability over an inexorably complex inventory network. Second, with increased desires around benefit quality combined with clients shopping both on the web and conventional channels, the reconciliation between discrete on the web and customary retail specialty units has turned out to be basically critical. Third, the request variances made by both unsurprising regular necessities and also unexpected strokes of luck can prompt inventory network interruption.

This is the place constant information investigation comes into the photo. In case you're ready to track and follow occasions over a siloed production network progressively, you accomplish end-to-end perceivability all through the inventory network and the spryness required to oversee both pinnacle necessities and surprising interruptions.

Put essentially, in case you're breaking down information afterward, you can't pinpoint issues and influence acclimations to sufficiently quick to avert missed conveyances and out-of-stock circumstances previously they affect the client. Be that as it may, when retailers can examine gushing information, they can improve expectations, choices and alterations progressively, before the client encounter is contrarily influenced.

How do gushing information investigation abilities enable vast scale retailers to enhance store network administration?

End-to-end perceivability and coordination all through the production network: As retail organizations develop, each extra store network connect additionally tangles the web through expanded interdependencies, siloed frameworks and correspondence holes. A gushing information investigation arrangement cannot just furnish a retailer with an up-to-the-moment and thorough perspective of all features of the inventory network, yet it can likewise give them a chance to gather, relate, break down and follow up on information from various sources and frameworks progressively.

How does this play out in this present reality? Suppose that you're working a fast serve eatery network and your squeezed orange provider misses a conveyance. In case you're investigating inventory network information sometime later, you get some answers concerning this issue when stores bring in to report being out-of-stock. In any case, if your production network administration arrangement incorporates spilling information examination capacities, you end up plainly mindful of the deferral progressively and your framework organizes a workaround arrangement to such an extent that operations and stock levels are undisrupted and clients stay cheerful.

Mix between omni-stream supply chains for conventional stores and online organizations

Retailers can depend on clients to be savvier and more particular than any other time in recent memory. Experts and INTERNATIONAL. Retail and Distribution Leader at world leading Consulting firm that creative retailers are centered around conveying a coordinated "omni-channel" involvement, perceiving that similar clients are shopping both on the web and in-store and that channel incorporation is vital for conveying the most ideal client encounter.

Retailers that are effectively handling this issue are outfitted with four capacities: 1) a conclusion to-end straightforward perspective of the production network crosswise over both conventional and online specialty units; 2) a capacity to distinguish and settle issues progressively before the client is affected; 3) a capacity to coordinate information from different, siloed sources crosswise over specialty units to offer steady administration levels ; and 4) a capacity to use authentic information to set baselines to better dissect spilling information to influence more to solid and auspicious forecasts.

Overseen variances popular

Customary production network administration approaches depend on chronicled information for stock arranging – and it's useful for arranged cycles and pinnacle necessities. In any case, recorded information isn't unpleasantly helpful for unexpected strokes of luck that have prompt effect on stock prerequisites.

On the off chance that you have continuous perceivability over your production network and can make acclimations to deal with the unforeseen, you can react to request changes progressively to address your clients' issues since you're operationally coordinated.

Executing constant information examination unfathomably enhances store network productivity, and imaginative retailers are utilizing these capacities to enhance inventory network administration crosswise over different operational useful zones. Ongoing examination abilities enhance determining and request arranging and better coordinate sourcing and generation operations. For stock administration crosswise over channels, continuous investigation joins specialty units and siloed frameworks to guarantee that things are unendingly in stock and conveyed immediately.

By the day's end, it's tied in with keeping the client glad and faithful through envisioning their necessities and reliably conveying the experience they anticipate. Furthermore, with ongoing examination, you're generally one stage ahead with retail store network administration.

Misener additionally gave a report on B2B2C pioneers's ramble conveyance program, Special Air

"I believe it's at last to the point where individuals don't come up to me and ask, is it genuine?" he stated, including he was the group that composed the automaton PR and FAQ years ahead of time, some portion of the organization's advancement DNA. "It's anything but difficult to get occupied by how cool the innovation is. This is an unfortunate chore, meeting the predicament of how to suit a client who needs a thing conveyed inside 30 minutes of their request. We've handled two-day and same-day conveyance; now it's that 30-minute hindrance. Clients ask themselves, 'Do I manage without it or bounce in my auto?' That's not a decent decision."

Misener said B2B2C pioneers is working intimately with the Federal Aviation Administration (FAA) on the best utilization of airspace, and has fused "sense and keep away from" frameworks to influence automaton to utilize safe. "This is something requiring a ton of administrative endorsement and open acknowledgment. We won't send them until the point when we can ensure open wellbeing. We've contracted previous military pilots and a previous space explorer."

He likewise said B2B2C pioneers developments like automaton propeller configuration have been utilized by others. The automatons themselves weigh under 55 lbs., can fly out up to 15 miles and convey things weighing up to 5 lbs., speaking to a "greater part of things" in B2B2C pioneers's stock.

"This is genuine – it's not simply batteries and toothpaste, but rather an entire host of things," he said.

The Perfect Customer Order Demands Perfect Execution

With regards to satisfaction, each web based business advanced installment arrangement can identify with the lion tamer's test.

Similarly as he or she should educate gigantic, hot-tempered creatures to react to orders without turning into their lunch, so should the web based business advanced installment arrangement get clients' products conveyed on time and in place — all while keeping costs from soaring. Obviously, internet business merchant s have a scarcely discernible difference to stroll to achieve first class satisfaction.

Going through the motions

With all the contending factors at play, satisfaction is a dubious situation that requires expertise, extremely quick turns and a calm attitude. From adjusting postage and bundling costs without climbing up the clients' cost to collecting huge amounts of requests crosswise over various deals channels into one succinct satisfaction stage, these unlimited snags can be hard to explore.

What's more, bear in mind the profits procedure, which can really begin to tackle your primary concern, at that point return to additionally frequent you as additional authoritative expenses. In the event that your stock isn't arranged and recorded accurately when those profits return to the distribution center, you're returned to with the agony of the nibble a moment time.

Over these essential online business dilemmas sits elevated client requests and desires. Customers need shorter handling windows; as time contends with cash, this reality turns into another benefit muncher.

"Ouch! The Corporate Sting of Fulfillment Challenges

At this point, you know satisfaction challenges aren't only an agony — they can genuinely trade off your business.

Each time you make a satisfaction slip, your primary concern endures a shot. You invest energy that ought to be possessed building different parts of your business, such as showcasing, marking and item improvement. What's more, those negative client encounters because of request delays, mis-boats, or poor correspondence? You can dare to dream they don't turn into a web sensation in surveys.

So what's a web based business advanced installment answer for do? The appropriate response can be summed up in single word: improve. Here's the secret:

Band together with the Best

Building associations with satisfaction accomplices that have solid innovation foundations ought to be a need. For the best outcomes, discover one encountered with brands and items that are like those you offer.

A strong satisfaction accomplice should comprehend what it's doing, while at the same time giving specialized know-how and straightforward valuing. Make certain to get some information about "concealed" expenses, for example, account support or tech costs. What's more, ensure any huge postage rebates the satisfaction accomplice gets are passed on in full to clients.

Have the Right Tools in Place

It's constantly about the apparatuses. In case you're not at a phase while outsourcing satisfaction bodes well, you require those devices much more. Scan for stages that will enable you to track your stock, send items at reduced rates and give full perceivability of information over all business channels. Endeavor to mechanize however much of the everyday work as could be expected, enabling you to oversee satisfaction on an abnormal state without superfluous diversions.

It's basic: Just Communicate

On the off chance that you don't need irate clients exploding your online networking, shield them from getting furious in any case by ensuring they know the status of their requests. For computerized installment arrangements pitching to the U.K., for example, U.K. law requires online business retailers to keep clients aware of everything with composed request confirmation. What's more, even where that is not the law, it's quite recently great business.

Clients value having cutting-edge arrange information so give them the capacity to see where their requests are through internet following frameworks, including any reports on changes or postponements. Regardless of the possibility that requests are later than anticipated, they'll never need to think about when their bundle is coming or get support to discover.

Internet business satisfaction is completely an animal requiring cautious taking care of. Be that as it may, similar to the lion tamer, internet business computerized installment arrangements can control satisfaction. Streamlining forms in house or with a trusted accomplice gives you a chance to concentrate on greater objectives without annoying your clients or putting your business in danger.

What Retailers Can Expect in current/not so distant future

Since current year is gone, I'd get a kick out of the chance to share our expectations on what current/not so distant future holds for the retail business. Following a time of developments for the purchaser encounter – see-now, purchase now to virtual fitting rooms – awesome items and moment satisfaction are the desire of customers. Purchasers need what they need, when and where they need it. Also, on the off chance that they don't get it, they're speedy to move onto the following brand who will give it.

The computerized upset has been changing the desires of customers for quite a long time, yet current year speaks to a genuine defining moment. It's not quite recently the blast of cool new gadgets or versatile shopping. In the New Retail Economy, social is above all else and it impacts everything – and not only our shopping propensities. We depend on social confirmation not just when we're perusing B2B2C pioneers or finding an extraordinary eatery on Yelp. Social apparatuses are crossing into proficient lives too – think corporate intranets, ambassador applications like Slack – changing the way business is done today. It's a very surprising model from the past, where business applications (consider the whole Office suite) in the long run streamed into the purchaser world. What's more, as retailers endeavor to meet buyers where they are, they're beginning to embrace devices and social inclinations that match their client base, and normally, the way the business runs changes.

Current/not so distant future: The Year of Social

Take the effect of interpersonal organizations. Retail is a space normally intended for these systems, as experts work in particular groups, or tribes – the various gatherings of planners, retailers, providers, factories, specialists and all the more every individual cooperates with day by day – to complete things.

For instance, creators work in one gathering to find and create ideas, and after that work with individuals in sourcing to make a completed item. Another tribe might be tapped to discover particular segments, catches, trim, materials to utilize, and accordingly work with store network accomplices, yet another tribe, to make sense of how to really manufacture and convey the item. People all through the retail group move from tribe to tribe in their business world a similar way they take advantage of their social groups in their purchaser lives: from Pinterest and Instagram to Snapchat and Facebook on their cell phones.

This tribal move is a defining moment for the business. The retail attitude is changing and new methodologies and methodologies are reinforcing the part's capacity to improve and make awesome item. To keep this going, current/not so distant future should be significantly more associated with their groups, requiring much greater interest in both front-end and back-end innovations to flourish.

Ways to Managed Shipping Costs

Mammoth omnichannel players, for example, marketplace, Bed Bath and Beyond, Tier 1 Imports and Hypermarket have brought down their free-transportation limits to better contend with B2B2C pioneers. While the huge computerized installment arrangements are paying for this to some

One more snap, and they were en route – for the win!

After two days, the shoes arrived by means of UPS. They fit splendidly – I needed to figure in the store, knocking up a half size – in the wake of utilizing a couple of substantial socks. Yet, the delivery box was something different once more:

Notwithstanding expounding on omnichannel, I've likewise composed broadly on dimensional weight estimating. This is the place the real transporters have changed their valuing equation for web based business packages to catch more income and balance the cost of delivery loads of air.

It's been a few years now since DIM was extended to incorporate all residential ground shipments by UPS and FedEx, and most computerized installment arrangements have balanced their transportation hones as needs be to reduce the wound up in a sorry situation line affect. Some basic practices incorporate utilizing custom box estimating machines that fit the bundle to the item, or on account of substantial volume shippers, arranging some alleviation as a custom DIM divisor.

The Latest Trends in Ecommerce Packaging and Their Impacts

The bundling you use in online business and direct-to-client shipments goes about as an envoy of your image. How it shows up, how it ensures the substance and even how the item is pressed can consider emphatically or contrarily your organization. Addressing the requirements of the present buyer implies remembering the experience when settling on choices on your bundling operations. However, in the meantime you have to watch your expenses and stay productive. This report will investigate ways that computerized installment arrangements are hoping to adjust these goals through development and the utilization of new frameworks and procedures. Download this MCM Operations Special Report and learn:

> How the utilization of movable tallness containers can diminish void fill and along these lines DIM charges and delivering costs

> How new frameworks empower the utilization of more grounded, better-fixing water-actuated tape in a creation situation

> How innovation propels like littler air cushion machines are empowering store-based satisfaction to look the same as your DC operation

> How changing more requests from folded boxes to polybags can have an immense effect on costs while looking after marking

Transportation/Delivery

MCM Outlook current/not so distant future: Seismic Shopping Shifts Bring
Evolution to Fulfillment

Move happens. What's more, at the present time, there's a seismic move in
how INTERNATIONAL. customers shop. Following quite a while of being
told by web based business examiners and specialists that "this is the Year of
Mobile," versatile trade is at last here, and it's taking the conventional retail
display with it.

Shoppers are never again quite recently setting off to the store and purchasing
what they require, and that is changing the way retailers do everything from
satisfying and transporting requests to speaking with and fulfilling their
clients.

In this MCM Outlook Special Report on Operations you will learn:

> Why a contracting store scene implies extraordinary open
> doors for omnichannel retailers

> How retailers are coordinating B2B2C pioneers's speed by
> delivery from stores

> Why purchase online pickup in store is seeing awesome
> development

> What's driving brought down free-delivery limits

6 Effective Steps to Create a Sustainable Shipping Environment

With expanding mindfulness about environmental change, an ever increasing
number of organizations are reexamining their natural impression. Those
in the transportation and coordinations parts are changing their inventory
network. The concentration is moving from expanded profitability to
improved maintainability remainder.

This conveys us to the significance of best transporting rehearses. While
picking the most recent delivery patterns, it is additionally fundamental to

see that they make your transportation condition more practical. Here are six compelling strides to enable you to assemble a feasible transportation condition:

Go Green with bundling materials

Reexamine the bundling materials your business employments. Polystyrene froth, paper marks, and so forth., are on the whole dangerous to nature and add to your carbon impression. Polystyrene froth is harmful to condition because of its deadly sythesis, and it takes several years to decay. Pick materials which are eco-accommodating, recyclable and practical. Folded cardboard is a standout amongst the most mainstream bundling material and furthermore the most reused. With regards to naming, warm printers are extraordinary compared to other condition amicable choices accessible. The warm names dispose of the requirement for ink and pressing tape if the present names need cement backing.

Is it the correct size?

Bigger than-required bundles are a standout amongst the most well-known blunders in transportation situations. They prompt assembling of pointless bundling material and fillers. What's more, the greater part of the fillers are neither reusable nor recyclable. Expansive boxes likewise consume up more room in transportation vehicles. This in the long run outcomes in expanded fuel use. Pack more quick witted to maintain a strategic distance from these disadvantages. Utilize devices, for example, mechanized box making machines, to fabricate consummate estimated boxes. Right-measure bundling spares you assets, cash, time, stockroom space, lessens item harm, and furthermore enhances the ecological main concern.

Weigh it right

It is critical that every one of the bundles are weighed precisely before transportation. Additionally, the stacked trucks ought to be weighed with great quality measuring scales, for example, truck scales. For the most part, it is fitting that the heaviness of each bundle ought not surpass 50 pounds, because of wellbeing reasons. On the off chance that regardless it exceeds, at that point such bundles ought to be plainly marked as needs be. In the event that the bundle contains beds, at that point the right weight is the gross weight of the item and bed joined. What's more, this joined weight ought not surpass 1,500 pounds. Every one of the bundles ought to be secured with fitting restricting materials.

Think Bulk

Distinguish every one of your clients who put orders for numerous items. For them, you can send every one of the items together in a similar holder. This will enable you to spare impressively on bundling materials. Numerous a times, in view of requests and their desperation, items are required to be delivered exclusively. Be that as it may, at whatever point you can, make it a point to dispatch in mass. This diminishes cargo space wastage and additionally fuel utilization.

Improve on Sustainability

To enhance the supportability of inventory network, you should first evaluate its execution. This empowers you to act particularly on the issue focuses, and devise important activity gets ready for the same. In the event that your shipment orders don't fill a whole truck or say a plane, you should pick co-shipping with different organizations. This can reasonably lessen fuel costs and furthermore help limit the ecological impression of your business. Set benchmarks towards a more manageable inventory network and include your workers. Since objectives are accomplished, better together.

Minimizing Waste

Run computerized with your printed material. This is a standout amongst the most critical strides to limit squander. There are various advanced cell applications accessible which upgrade profitability while additionally boosting the 'green remainder' of your stockroom operations. You can practically accomplish zero printed material. The gear can be related with electronic mark which permits accuracy following of the shipment and also safeguard affirmation on conveyance. Accordingly, you will be granted with an additional preferred standpoint of quicker charging and enhanced income.

Instill these ways and amplify the profitability of your distribution center. You will enhance the earth and benefits to your business without a doubt.

Goal Determines Favorite Shippers in B2B World

When it comes down to which divide transporter is a most loved in the B2B world, the appropriate response should be, "residential shipper or global shipper?" as per discoveries from Omni Stream Idealogies.

At the point when asked which distribute was their essential local bearer, about portion of all the B2B reviewed said the United Postal Service (44.5%), arriving in a far off second was FedEx with a fourth of the reactions, at that point United States Postal Service with 14.5%, and FedEx Smartpost with 1.8%. Pretty much 14% of respondents recorded "Other" as their essential residential bearer which incorporated different reactions of a split amongst UPS and FedEx, flatbed trucks, and different LTL transporters.

"The development of FedEx First Overnight will enable us to keep on meeting the developing interest of business-to-business clients requiring auspicious, and "Regardless of whether it's a human services organization making arrangements for an early morning surgery or an assembling office needing a basic part to anticipate downtime logistic clients esteem speed, security and perceivability, which FedEx First Overnight gives, making it less demanding for them to concentrate on dealing with their business."

"While the choice to support UPS makes various focuses, the most noteworthy of this choice is its effect in protecting an aggressive domain in Europe by clearing up the methodology and important criteria for merger endorsement," UPS said in an announcement.

B2B and IoT Jargon: the Future of IoT and Retail

Cost reserve funds assume a noteworthy part in the IoT informing of significant programming sellers. Be that as it may, in a current review, retailers esteemed IoT information investigation as an approach to enhance marketing, not operations. What's going on, and what does IoT information investigation offer retailers?

Overview Emphasizes Differentiation, Consumer Pricing

In a previous year overview directed by Boston-based Retail Systems Research, retailers were asked which difficulties would influence them to consider IoT answers for their stores.

Given cost-, edge and development based difficulties, retailers picked development. They gave top an incentive to IoT information examination to enable them to oversee development related difficulties. Separating their brands and observing customer value affectability were their top of the line utilizes for IoT.

B2B and IoT Jargon: Data Analytics Technologies for Retailers

All in all, what does IoT intend to retailers? Present day innovation gives us a few approaches to cut, dice and break down retail information. The distinctions lie in information volume, speed of examination and where the information originates from.

Technology	What it does	What it delivers	Capabilities
Big data analytics	Uses high-speed, high-volume data handling methods and tools. Analyzes stored data.	Turns huge volumes of data into actionable information.	Can handle a wide variety of data such as database records, images, emails and digital documents.
Fast data analytics	Uses big data technology and tools on smaller data volumes. Mines raw, stored data in real time.	Information that retailers can use immediately to change prices or improve customer experience.	Avoids the delay in analysis and visualization of big data analytics.
IoT data analytics	Automatically gathers and analyzes streaming data from connected sources such as mobile phones, POS, video cameras and social media.	Actionable information on customer preferences, products, pricing and the competition.	Provides up-to-the-minute customer responses to prices, trends, in-store events and sales.

Associated with a system and the web, these IT assets assume a fundamental part in IoT information examination:

> IoT resources, for example, portable and associated gadgets, sensors and reference points. These assemble spilling information and course it to the retailer organize.

> Data stockpiling, which gives business clients and experts access to colossal volumes of chronicled information.

> Data investigation programming, which with regards to retail examination can be utilized to break down and picture gushing information, set computerized alarms and robotize report dissemination and booking.

> Data investigation stages, which can be situated on-premises or in the cloud. This brought together computerized workspace forms IoT data accumulated from many focuses on the web and conveys noteworthy data to clients.

Here are a couple of cases of how retailers can utilize these advantages for screen costs and separate their image.

Watching out for Consumer Price Changes

Numerous studies and respondents were occupied with utilizing IoT information investigation to gage buyer value affectability. Business clients can do this with IoT information depictions or set up and test evaluating methodologies.

Screen client reaction to value changes

Measuring client responses to late retail value changes is a then-versus-now examination. Business clients can contrast deals volumes related with put away information or data hot off the IoT wire. In any case, IoT innovation makes it simple to assemble, investigate, envision and offer data consequently.

Test a current value procedure

Making or refreshing your evaluating methodology is another approach to utilize value affectability data assembled on the IoT.

When you set up a factually substantial test, you'll ensure that evaluating is in accordance with your plan of action and target gathering of people. The speed of continuous, gushing information examination makes a progression of consider the possibility that tests simple to set up, assess and utilize.

In the event that you require more than one system, startup is simple. You'll most likely begin gathering information from POS and numerous different gadgets you haven't approached some time recently.

By utilizing IoT stage and programming abilities, you can locate the best item value go for particular groups of onlookers. Study client purchasing designs; IoT information get-together, investigation and sharing are programmed.

Utilizing IoT to Make Your Brand Distinctive

Study respondents additionally saw the IoT information investigation as an amazing approach to separate their brands. What better route for your business to separate itself as a place to get incredible costs, a flavorful client encounter—or both?

At the point when Numbers Rule: Differentiating by Price

Speed and dexterity are the fundamental focal points of IoT information investigation. You can accumulate information from numerous areas and gadgets, screen current conditions, change costs and test client conduct rapidly and frequently.

Utilize IoT information to gauge deals conduct of focused groups of onlookers previously, then after the fact particular value changes. You'll find rapidly whether a particular group of onlookers acknowledges that 10-percent cost increment. On the off chance that you don't win out over the competition? You can react rapidly without putting a genuine gouge into incomes.

Making Your Mark with Support Services

At the point when it's troublesome or difficult to separate on value, despite everything you have choices. Numerous re-digital-payments set their business apart by including esteem included administrations, for example, quicker dispatching, free returns or an amusing to-utilize versatile application that realizes what you like.

IoT adds to quick delivering by social affair RFID information off your bundles and sending it to following programming in your coordinations focus. On the off chance that clients restore their merchandise, you'll most likely have put away individual and item data that causes you make sense of what turned out badly.

Furthermore, that cell phone application? More about that underneath.

Developing Personalized Shopping Experiences

IoT likewise enables retailers to utilize client inclination and conduct information to make solid, long haul connections. Here are a few cases of IoT innovation and how it makes engaging shopping encounters.

> Use cell phones to make clients glad. Enable your clients to locate their most loved items and brands at your store, not down the road. Furnish their cell phones with applications loaded with your store data. They can scan for what they need, find out about deals and audit in-store occasions with their companions. Utilize reference points to alarm enrolled clients about their most loved items and administrations.

> Make one of a kind item proposals. When you track client inclinations and get acquainted with their purchasing propensities, utilize that back-end information to distinguish likely future buys. Track singular tastes, past buys and faithfulness focuses to give recommendations and costs that interest to every client.

Improve items and administrations. Accumulate in-store
criticism or online networking streams to change items
in view of direct client reactions and area information.

IoT Advantages: Speed, Agility and Lower Risk

With IoT information examination, retailers can rapidly assemble, break
down, picture and utilize tremendous volumes of information from numerous
gadgets. Despite the fact that this may influence your IT master's heart to
vacillate, there's a lot of offer from a business perspective:

Reduce showcase chance. Spilling IoT information
encourages you know, not think about what's occurring
at the present time. Furthermore, you can roll out
improvements and distinguish openings rapidly before
your market changes.

Avoid costs. You can test hunches without committing
exorbitant business errors.

Control costs. Albeit new, IoT innovation needn't bust your financial plan.
Accessible as a cloud-based administration, IoT information investigation is
frequently offered as a month to month membership benefit.

Pick UP & Drop OFF

BIGGYBOX, e-commerce delivery arm of DEALS, has planned with logistic-based company PICKUP services to convert hundreds of outlets into pickup and delivery points for e-commerce companies across ASEAN. The last mile delivery of goods is a challenge for most e-commerce companies and DEALS joins others such as dealers to offer specific outlets for firms such as gas station and retails shops to drop goods for their consumers.

Deals is working hard to provide both consumers and sellers pick up and drop off points for easier transactions and instant access to the products and services provided on our site. When you place an order or need to fulfill an order for your customers using BIGGYBOX.COM admin panel provides an excellent order summaries page where you will be able to schedule delivery or pick up instead of just the standard home delivery option. BIGGYBOX.COM is partnering with different small shops, warehouses and gas stations as drop off and pick up spots for your convenience. Whether you use Deals for selling or buying products there are more options available to you today through BIGGYBOX.COM partnerships with these sites throughout the ASEAN region. Using our order summaries page is very simple and you choose how you want to deliver and pick up your orders with a simple click of a button.

Quick and expert request satisfaction is what is required in the present web based business showcase. Arrangements give their vendors mass import and fare of items and administrations that are effectively overseen and easy to get it. BIGGYBOX.COM is an incredible web based business stage that takes into consideration venders and purchasers to effortlessly transfer and download clients, dealers, items and requests alongside picking how to pay and where to get and convey the items and administrations. Arrangements accomplices with ASEAN district shops and different areas for helpful get and drop off destinations all through the whole traverse of the locale. With these components Deals give their vendors exceptional administrations and devices to convey just expert client benefit, installment alternatives and get and drop off areas to every one of their clients and merchants that will abandon them glad and satisfied

BIGGYBOX.COM platform allows merchants to build beautiful store fronts that will attract more customers. Deals provide several different options when building and maintaining a professional looking site through their

BIGGYBOX.COM admin portal. The admin portal has components such as slides to add to your ecommerce site, banners, easy navigation tools, standard static HTML pages, blogs and blog posts, different themes and file storage. After you create your store front you are provided teams of experts to help you with your marketing, payment options and pick up and drop off sites throughout the ASEAN region. With the pick up and drop off sites throughout the region there is no reason to worry when the customers pour in and you are having numerous delivery and fulfillment requirements. BIGGYBOX.COM provides professional sites for all your ecommerce store front needs and experts in the distribution and fulfillment category

At BIGGYBOX.COM you have many options on your stores settings that you can customize per your unique requirements. The settings include general type settings such as logos and store name, personal site address, shipping options, different payment options and methods, user registration and functions and social media links for enhanced engagement. Deals offer multiple admins and through the admin portal you can setup your email notifications, taxes, SSL certificates, currencies, methods of shipments and much more. BIGGYBOX. COM has 'Pick up and Drop off' spots throughout the ASEAN region for the convenience of our sellers and buyers. Throughout the region Deals has partnerships with gas stations, warehouses and shops where you can set up a complete fulfillment and distribution supply chain.

Using Deals you can set up your store with multiple sellers and each seller can be managed through the seller settings section of the admin portal. BIGGYBOX.COM allows for their merchants to invite multiple sellers to sell products and services on their site which allows for larger organic traffic which may lead to larger conversions of your products and services. Deals provides their merchants with many different distribution and selling settings such as themed sites, payment methods and pick up and drop off locations throughout the ASEAN region. If you have a multi-seller marketplace then these delivery and pick up locations will provide a full scale distribution solution for each of your sellers. Gone are the days of customers allowing weeks to fulfill an order and Deals fulfillment options of pick up and drop off locations allow for your sellers to meet the needs of their consumers

BIGGYBOX.COM provides their merchants with many different shipment options. In the admin portal merchants can manage their order shipments in the shipping section. Deals partners with ASEAN region shops, gas stations and logistic companies to make shipping and receiving easier. Throughout the region streamlined pick up and drop off locations are available for the convenience of customers and sellers. Both customers and sellers are no longer satisfied with age old shipping methods and the advanced drop off and pick up locations make the distribution and fulfillment component much quicker and easier.

Summary

I have share a lot in here And with a lot of friends But to also making and running profitable business for a coffee from social media, you need to see it as a serious business. This book gives you a few powerful principles and strategies on how a online storefront business can be create with profitable results. So start building a little cozy E-business and making useful of social media and enjoy unlimited income Or grow as entrepreneur, this is fun and profitable!

Learn and incorporate the simplest basic principles of business into your passionate online storefront or e-commerce activity and turn it into a real activity and income stream at the same time.

Everyone dreams of financial independence. If you seek a second income stream, some extra money for a little luxury, then this book shows you how money is made ecommerce. See a handful of lucrative strategies and solutions that will help build a successful business from the very beginning and avoid costly unsuccessful action. It will help you cut the time before getting in business for real, too.

All the basics of a small business are explained in this book, so you can share your masterpiece with everybody and also make a living out of it.

Grab this book and start making a revenue with ecommerce businesse today!

Printed in the United States
By Bookmasters